Praise for *Understanding Y...*

In order to get to true equity, we must shift fr...
practices to thinking about instructional pow...
instructional power, as Reed Marshall outlines...
to think differently about their impact on students in service of developing their
agency to become powerful independent learners.

> — **Zaretta Hammond**, teacher educator and author of
> *Culturally Responsive Teaching and the Brain*

Dr. Tanji Reed Marshall lands a seminal read that is not to be missed!
Understanding Your Instructional Power is a unique teacher-oriented book that
addresses instruction within the context of power and the impact of teachers'
power on students' learning and perceptions of self. The Power Principle matrix
should be taught in every teacher training program because it masterfully depicts
the power teachers have in instructional decision making—from empowering
to disenfranchising. As a former teacher, I appreciate how Dr. Reed Marshall
empowers teachers to unleash their skills and knowledge to make a lasting
difference in the education of students. This is an important book!

> — **Cheryl Holcomb-McCoy**, PhD, Dean and Distinguished Professor,
> School of Education, American University

Understanding Your Instructional Power is a brilliant, thoughtful, and practical book
designed to guide teachers in believing in and modeling the power of powerful
and empowering thinking for themselves and their students. Vignettes, activities,
and concrete examples guide teachers in fostering empowered/empowering
environments where students' learning is authentic, culturally responsive, and
rigorous. I am excited about the promise of this masterful work at helping teachers
to be more effective professionals overall, and especially with minoritized students.

> — **Donna Y Ford**, PhD, Distinguished Professor of Education
> and Human Ecology, The Ohio State University

Feeling frustrated by your lack of power? In *Understanding Your Instructional
Power*, Tanji Reed Marshall demonstrates how teachers actually possess
tremendous power to influence the trajectory of their students' learning—for
better and for worse. She urges practitioners to reflect upon how they wield this
power in terms of both curricular decision making as well as in their minute-by-
minute decision making in the classroom. Reed Marshall makes clear that teaching
responsibly and ethically is a moral imperative.

> — **Carol Jago**, English teacher, past president of the
> National Council of Teachers of English, and board member
> of the International Literacy Association

Teachers have tremendous power over whether, what, and how students learn.
While teachers aim to use that power for good, unexamined cultural differences
with their students can lead teachers to inadvertently misuse their power to ill
effect. In this useful volume, Reed Marshall mines her rich experience in schools
and uses an approachable style to illustrate how power regularly interferes with
teaching and learning and to guide readers in self-examining and transforming the
influence they have on their students.

> — **Jill Harrison Berg**, EdD, author of *Uprooting Instructional Inequity:
> The Power of Inquiry-Based Professional Learning*

Knowing, understanding, and intentionally using one's instructional power is essential for equitable, high-quality teaching and learning. Thank you, Dr. Tanji Reed Marshall, for the reminder of how we as educators hold the professional privilege of changing students' lives in each moment of planning, preparation, and execution in our day-to-day moments as teachers. *Understanding Your Instructional Power* is essential reading for teachers and leaders at any career stage.

— **Lacey Robinson**, president and CEO, UnboundEd

Tanji Reed Marshall skillfully holds a mirror up for teachers and encourages them to be brave enough to closely examine who they are and how that shapes the decisions they make and the level of agency and empowerment students experience in their classrooms. Her book creates many pause to reflect opportunities for school district leaders and principals to examine their role in creating the conditions for teachers to explore the dimensions of power that shape their decision making. An unpacking of the implications of the Power Principle matrix should be integrated into all professional learning opportunities for teachers and leaders in a school district!

— **Ann Blakeney Clark**, former teacher, principal, and school district superintendent

Dr. Tanji Reed Marshall not only exposes how power dynamics in the classroom disrupt a child's education but also provides a clear, impactful guide to help teachers make effective decisions throughout the school day. Any teacher who uses *Understanding Your Instructional Power* will tremendously improve their teaching and student relationships. I look forward to seeing the results Reed Marshall's work will have on our nation's schools.

— **Sharif El-Mekki**, CEO, Center for Black Educator Development

Tanji Reed Marshall's book takes me back to 8th grade when I found my voice and became empowered to speak my truth. Only one teacher, Mr. Lovelace, empowered my agency through high expectations and a meaningful partnership with my family. Reed Marshall breaks down in realistic and tangible ways how, with deep self-awareness and acknowledgement of power, teachers can shift classroom cultures from *protective* and *disenfranchising* to *agentive* and *empowering*.

— **Nancy B. Gutierrez**, EdLD, president and CEO, The Leadership Academy

How are my actions affecting students? The many answers to this question have significant implications for teachers' abilities to support student learning and make schools the equitable spaces they have yet to become. *Understanding Your Instructional Power* offers a carefully researched rationale for the importance of unpacking power and provides a road map that can help teachers examine their relationships with power and consider how it influences their actions—and how those actions shape students' lives.

— **Trevor Thomas Stewart**, PhD, program leader for English education, Virginia Tech

Understanding Your

INSTRUCTIONAL
POWER

ASCD MEMBER BOOK

Many ASCD members received this book as a
member benefit upon its initial release.

Learn more at: **www.ascd.org/memberbooks**

Understanding Your
INSTRUCTIONAL
POWER

*Curriculum and Language Decisions
to Support Each Student*

Tanji Reed Marshall

Arlington, Virginia USA

2800 Shirlington Road, Suite 1001 • Arlington, VA 22206 USA
Phone: 800-933-2723 or 703-578-9600 • Fax: 703-575-5400
Website: www.ascd.org • Email: member@ascd.org
Author guidelines: www.ascd.org/write

Penny Reinart, *Deputy Executive Director;* Genny Ostertag, *Managing Director, Book Acquisitions & Editing;* Susan Hills, *Senior Acquisitions Editor;* Mary Beth Nielsen, *Interim Director, Book Editing;* Liz Wegner, *Editor;* Thomas Lytle, *Creative Director;* Donald Ely, *Art Director;* Lindsey Smith/The Hatcher Group, *Graphic Designer;* Cynthia Stock, *Typesetter;* Kelly Marshall, *Production Manager;* Shajuan Martin, *E-Publishing Specialist*

All web links in this book are correct as of the publication date below but may have become inactive or otherwise modified since that time. If you notice a deactivated or changed link, please email books@ascd.org with the words "Link Update" in the subject line. In your message, please specify the web link, the book title, and the page number on which the link appears.

PAPERBACK ISBN: 978-1-4166-3145-3   ASCD product #122027
PDF E-BOOK ISBN: 978-1-4166-3146-0; see Books in Print for other formats.
Quantity discounts are available: email programteam@ascd.org or call 800-933-2723, ext. 5773, or 703-575-5773. For desk copies, go to www.ascd.org/deskcopy.

ASCD Member Book No. FY23-5 (Feb. 2023 P). ASCD Member Books mail to Premium (P), Select (S), and Institutional Plus (I+) members on this schedule: Jan, PSI+; Feb, P; Apr, PSI+; May, P; Jul, PSI+; Aug, P; Sep, PSI+; Nov, PSI+; Dec, P. For current details on membership, see www.ascd.org/membership.

Library of Congress Cataloging-in-Publication Data
Names: Reed Marshall, Tanji, author.
Title: Understanding your instructional power : curriculum and language
    decisions to support each student / Tanji Reed Marshall.
Description: Arlington, Virginia : ASCD, 2023. | Includes bibliographical
    references and index.
Identifiers: LCCN 2022027922 (print) | LCCN 2022027923 (ebook) | ISBN
    9781416631453 (paperback) | ISBN 9781416631460 (pdf)
Subjects: LCSH: Teacher-student relationships. | Motivation in education.
Classification: LCC LB1033 .R454 2023 (print) | LCC LB1033 (ebook) | DDC
    371.102/3—dc23/eng/20220719
LC record available at https://lccn.loc.gov/2022027922
LC ebook record available at https://lccn.loc.gov/2022027923

32 31 30 29 28 27 26 25 24 23   1 2 3 4 5 6 7 8 9 10 11 12

This book is dedicated to my students,
who are the impetus for this book.
Thank you!

Understanding Your INSTRUCTIONAL POWER

PREFACE

Welcome to my sandbox! I'm thrilled to have you take a journey I took many years ago that, although tough, made me a better teacher, coach, and educator.

I came into education as a second career through an alternative-route program that was one of the best in my state. It prepared me for nearly everything I would encounter in the classroom—except one thing: it did not tell me about the tremendous power I would have to shape the lives of the students who would be assigned to me. It did not help me understand how who I was as a person was among the most impactful elements that would shape how I interacted with my students. I had to learn those lessons the hard way, over many years of making decisions, watching my students, and reflecting on what I learned.

This book is about taking a journey of self-discovery to help you make critical connections between who you are, how you approach the world, and how the intersections of your background, upbringing, and worldview affect your classroom decisions. It is estimated that teachers make 1,500 decisions every day, each one imbued with a web of factors that can have positive and negative results for students. It is time to stop and begin to deeply examine what goes into those decisions, and that's what this book is intended to help you do.

Although you might read this book on your own, I would encourage you to invite one or more colleagues to join you; doing so could change your entire school for the better. At times you might need to take a break. Feel free to do so, but be sure to come back and complete the exercises in the Pause to Reflect sections.

1 | UNCOVERING YOUR INSTRUCTIONAL POWER

1,500 . . . 4

If you've ever read *Time* magazine, you've seen the "For the Record" page that shows a number or percent and explains its significance. The number is usually associated with some historic or outrageous event or comment that went viral in a ridiculously short time. Well, *1,500* and *4* are our "For the Record" numbers:

- For the Record: The average teacher makes 1,500 educational decisions every day.
- For the Record: The average teacher makes an educational decision every 4 minutes.

These numbers are based on research from the 1980s and 1990s, and they may be too low, given increasing demands placed on teachers today (Klein, 2021). Whether it's 1,500 or more, it's no wonder we're exhausted! When I was in the classroom, I never stopped to think about the number of decisions I made; I simply made them and "kept it moving."

If you've never considered the number of educational decisions you make in a day, now is the time to do so, because wrapped up in those decisions is tremendous power. I know, *power* is a word teachers rarely use, and it's something they rarely see themselves as possessing. However, if you're making an educational decision that affects anyone other than yourself, then not only do you have power; you've exercised that power in positive and negative ways. As shared in the Preface, this book is designed to help you pause and consider the various factors that contribute to your instructional power so you will use it to develop students' agency and empower them to join you in their quest to become educated, no matter where they—and you—happen to be on the journey.

Perceptions of Powerlessness

Most teachers, when asked, will likely tell you they do not have power or they do not see themselves as powerful. This perception persists despite a recent uptick in teacher strikes across the United States that have led to higher pay, increased school funding, and promises for more school counselors and nurses. The increased activism was not limited to traditionally Democratic states with strong teachers unions. In fact, teachers from districts engaged in protests and strikes exercised a level of activism and power unseen in modern times (Wolf, 2019). Although the activism increased teachers' understanding of their power to force change, the concept of *instructional* power remains unfamiliar to them. In my discussions and work with teachers about their views on their power, I've learned that many feel as though their power stops at the schoolhouse door and they're trapped under the weight of mandated curricula and instructional practices that leave them feeling anything but powerful. However, as you will see, a great deal of power rests within the pages of a curriculum and the boxes on instructional checklists, and teachers wield it in myriad ways.

Authority Versus Power

Before we talk about the power we wield as teachers, we must talk about the authority we have. Our power stems from our authority to do the job we've chosen and been licensed to do. The process of passing those exams and becoming licensed gives us the authority to execute our duties as educators.

The terms *authority* and *power* are often used interchangeably, and there is certainly an argument to do so; however, for the purposes of our work, I like to think of them as close cousins. I explain the difference between authority and power this way: "Authority exists according to one's role, position, and function, and power maintains the levers" (Reed Marshall & Seawood, 2019, p. 139).

Authority is bestowed upon you by a person or an entity (such as the state) to perform the duties associated with your position. There is an understanding that any job you hold carries with it a certain amount of positional authority that allows you to perform your task and make related decisions to control the operational aspects of the job and to ensure it is executed as expected. Consider this: your principal, based on the scope of their job and the associated expectations, has authority that you do not have to make decisions about matters related to your school, and you are bound by such decisions even when you disagree or think they are foolish. Your principal outranks you and is therefore allowed and expected to make decisions not afforded to you simply because of job title and function.

Power is what Beverly Tatum (1997) calls "the smog in the air" (p. 6). It's an intangible force that moves and governs the dynamics in and around every relationship. Power is about dimensions of control and the ability to get people to yield their will to yours.

Consider the following. Because you're a teacher, you've been ascribed authority, and because of that authority, you're expected to exercise the power associated with your role. In fact, you and your students have a tacit agreement that because you each sit in different seats in this schooling process, you will lead and they will follow— for the most part. Your students are keenly aware of the authority differences between you and them. They recognize the power differential associated with your being a teacher and their being students. Students expect you, their teacher, to exercise a certain amount of power in accordance with your authority. They've conceded a certain amount of individual power precisely because they understand the dynamics of the relationship. What they do not want is for their teachers to abuse this power; and believe me, when they recognize such abuse, they do *not* take it lying down.

The issue is not whether educators have power or not; the issue is what Nyberg (1981) explains as the erroneous need in our society to behave as though education and those in its business are devoid of a structure inherent in society as a whole. Education is treated as though the naturally occurring power structures do not or should not exist simply because women are the predominant arbiters and children are the receivers. As Nyberg attests, power dynamics govern every aspect of the relationships in education, as they do in every other structure in society. We must examine our beliefs about this need to cast education as a pure field protected from the fangs of power, but that undertaking is for another day. Let's agree, as members of society endowed with authority to tinker around in the minds of other people's children, that we have and exercise power in varying degrees and ways. The ways we exercise our power are governed by our ideologies, which have been shaped by our lived experiences.

Authority and Power in the Classroom

The classroom is a teacher's domain. It is where we have the most control and wield the most power (Pace & Hemmings, 2007). If you're like me, I'm sure you've subscribed to the "just let me shut my door and teach" philosophy, because the classroom is where you knew you could engage in the work you'd become a teacher to do. You knew you would be able to act in the best interest of your students despite the rules, regulations, and mandates that come and go with every new administration. Let's spend some time unpacking our classroom-power ideologies to get a sense of how we understand our power on a deeper level.

Remember the *1,500* and *4* at the beginning of this chapter? Well, this is where those 1,500 decisions (one every 4 minutes) take place—within the four walls of the classroom and affecting the students assigned to you. Consider this: schools are the only place where the primary "customers"—in this case, the students—have the least amount of say in what happens with and to them. Each year for 12 years, teachers and students enter into a relationship, and neither has a say in being assigned to the other. And each year, both (for the most part) comply with this system. It's quite remarkable, actually. This is perhaps the only relationship with so much on the line where neither party is consulted about being connected to the other. However, because each knows how the system works, they agree that teachers will lead and students will follow. One will teach, and the other will learn. We all know our place in this thing called schooling, and we play it well—that is, until we don't.

The classroom is the proving ground for teachers' ideologies. It is where, despite what teachers say they believe, their actions will offer evidence of what they actually believe. Consider the teachers who say they treat every student fairly, but who, upon observation, demonstrate favoritism for the girls by calling on them first to answer questions. How about the teachers who say they believe every child can be successful only to demonstrate low expectations for Black students by not providing adequate wait time or not always repeating the students' answers to confirm understanding? Such behaviors can be explained away, but as we will discuss throughout this book, they demonstrate a use of instructional power that disenfranchises students and negatively affects learning, connectivity, and students' identity as learners.

Teachers and Power

Anderson (1987) confirms the notion that teachers demonstrate power in their domain of control: the classroom. This is where teachers are most likely to be seen as leaders. Certainly, teachers are leaders in myriad other contexts; however, the classroom, where they are responsible for designing and orchestrating learning experiences, is where their leadership is most evident. It is there teachers set the culture, direct the interactions between students, and set the rules and procedures for governance.

As a classroom teacher, I was not big on rules, but I was big on procedures. I had procedures for entry, exit, setting up collaborative seating, turning in work—you name it, I had a procedure for it. This is how I began to help my students understand the culture of the classroom. Of course, I involved students in rule setting; but for the most part, like many teachers, the final rules were mine to advance. I was the adult, they were the children, and this was how the game was to be played.

When teachers think about power and authority, they tend to relegate their understanding to classroom management (Anderson, 1987; Pace & Hemmings, 2007). Classroom management is where traditional notions of adult authority make the most sense. It's easy to see through this lens. School is the place where young people are meant to learn how to become productive members of society

(Apple, 1982). Essentially, school is the nation's socializing entity. It functions to reproduce the structures of society and hold those structures in place. School operates as an agent of the society and acts to advance its ideals, principles, and values. Therefore, it is the job of teachers to ensure students learn acceptable knowledge and what it means to interact in society.

When students step too far out of line or exhibit behaviors too far beyond what society would expect or accept, teachers work to address the issue by managing students' behavior to get them back to the norm. They use the power of the pen to refer; they remove students by sending them to a colleague or to the school office.

Such moves are forms of power, which can fall under the auspices of managing classroom behavior; however, these actions reinforce the idea that students must behave in societally acceptable ways or they will face consequences. Although this lens is common, it is important to understand that authority associated with body control is a limited perspective on what power is and how it operates.

Not only is classroom management the primary lens through which many teachers understand their authority; the ability to control a classroom, particularly in certain settings, is seen as a badge of honor. Consider the teacher for whom managing the class is not a strong suit. That teacher is viewed with disapproval. I'm guilty of having given the side-eye to many teachers whose management style left what I considered to be "a lot to be desired." The ability to maintain order is emblematic of being a good teacher.

I'm reminded of the words of a principal I consulted with many years ago. He took me around his building to give me the lay of the land, and he framed descriptions of his teachers around his views on their classroom management skills. His thinking was that if teachers could not "control" the class, there was little room for them to teach. This is a common belief, and I will not spend time disputing its merits. However, I will say this principal did what many building leaders do: they understand teachers' abilities through the lens of behavior control as being even more critical, depending on the student demographics, than instructional practice.

Having more classes on behavior management is one of the top requests from new teachers when asked about their teacher prep courses (Orr et al., 1999). New teachers wish they had been given more guidance on how to manage behavior and control students. This need for more knowledge and practice with managing students is particularly salient in situations with racial differences between students and teachers. Studies have demonstrated that White teachers feel less prepared for classroom management when their students are primarily students of color and even more so when their students are Black than when their students are White or Asian (Douglas et al., 2008; Sleeter, 2008). This means White teachers feel ill-equipped to control their students of color, particularly their Black students, because they are not getting what they deem as sufficient amounts of guidance on this topic. Lacking the types of management skills needed to establish a productive classroom, many White teachers are more likely to resort to punitive measures to address what they consider to be inappropriate behavior from their students of color than they would with their White and Asian students.

So, when we talk about power, what are we to understand? How are we to conceptualize it? At its most basic, power usually involves imposing one's will over another to direct thought or behavior (Freire, 1985). When people enact their power, they tend to act from places of difference where advantage offers the ability to impose one's will over another either explicitly or implicitly.

Several factors determine power differentials that govern most, if not all, relationships. Chief among these differentials is position or job role. We understand this differential quite easily because it tends to be most prominent in our adult lives. If you're a teacher, you know that your principal is positionally above you; therefore, you probably have been in a situation where, simply because job function gives the principal more authority, you've been asked to do something you did not believe was in your students' best interests. You did not agree; you may have even voiced opposition. However, you most likely complied with what you were asked to do because the person asking or providing the directive was positionally above you. If you're a building leader, you've experienced a similar situation from your superintendent or principal leader, depending on your district's size and structure.

Layers of Power

Teachers are responsible for the learning environment and the learning, with inherent levels of authority that comes with such responsibility. We can see the teacher-student relationship through the lens of power layers. It's like an onion, with layer upon layer of power dynamics shaping and moving the relational imbalance.

Many factors create this imbalance, chief of which has a lot to do with the *in loco parentis* principle. Like many U.S. customs, in loco parentis was borrowed from the English system. It simply means "instead of a parent"—that is, once children are in the physical custody of their school, the school takes responsibility for them in place of their parents/caregivers. The principle harkens back to 1769, when Sir William Blackstone "asserted that part of parental authority is delegated to schoolmasters," as he believed "parents delegate to schoolmasters the powers of 'restraint and correction' that may be necessary to educate their children" (DeMitchell, 2015, p. 1). At the time of Blackstone's instituting what became education law, schooling of children was the sole responsibility of the local community, not the parents. In abiding by such a law, parents transferred educative care to their child's teacher.

This principle remains law and undergirds a primary understanding of how school operates. Schools assume responsibility to act for the well-being of children once they are physically in the care of their schools. This principle gives teachers acting parental rights of sorts to act on behalf of the child. One thing I would tell my students on a regular basis is this: "Your parents have given me the ability to act in their stead. They expect me to take care of you while you're in my class." It was something in which I took great pride because I knew I would act for my students the same way I would act for my biological children. My students did not always appreciate my acting in the place of their parents, but they eventually came to realize I was, indeed, acting *for* and not against them.

Wrapped within the in loco parentis principle is the age differential. Teachers are older than their students, and there is an inherent, pervasive belief that children are to give their elders a certain amount of respect regardless of how the adult treats or interacts with the child. Unfortunately, many teachers hold fast to the belief that students must respect them simply because they are older. This belief, coupled with the in loco parentis principle, rests at the center of how many teachers deal with their beliefs about power and their relationship to children.

Behavior management is another layer under the in loco parentis umbrella. Responsibility for child safety is a critical element of schooling. Children must be physically safe, and just as parents work to keep their children safe at home, adults in schools work to keep children physically safe in their buildings. Keeping children safe necessitates having procedures and structures to manage behavior. Teachers must use their state-ascribed authority to ensure a safe learning environment for all students. Make no mistake, effective management structures are essential for learning, because it is a rare student who learns well or even likes being in a disorderly classroom. Issues arise, however, when management veers into control and is meted out unfairly and rooted in unresolved biases and prejudices. (We'll talk more about this in the next chapter.)

Perhaps the most significant power layer is a teacher's primary job function: helping students learn material or gain skills they most often do not know or have. Teachers have long been seen as the primary source of knowledge (Cornelius & Herrenkohl, 2004), especially with very young children. Although it is widely known that children are not *tabula rasa* (blank slates), teachers are still viewed as the primary vehicle through which children acquire school-based knowledge and skills.

Being responsible for learning and developing children's minds is a weighty prospect, and with the increasing demands placed on teachers, assuming responsibility for children in place of their parents/caregivers creates a sense of power that goes beyond caring for the children in their stead. Such a responsibility can easily shift toward a sense of superiority if left unchecked. Coupling such a belief system with unresolved issues of racism and bias can lead to a perceived knowledge differential that becomes a dangerous power layer with which many students contend. If teachers believe their students come to them lacking knowledge, they will use what Freire (1970) has called a "banking method," whereby they treat children like empty piggy banks whose knowledge will come only from the all-knowing teacher. Seeing students through this lens will manifest in language such as "these kids know nothing," and teachers will see part of their job as being the sole dispenser of knowledge without regard for what the child may know or bring to the learning environment.

Embedded within this layer is the positional dynamic between teachers and students. As the understood leaders in the classroom, teachers hold positional authority over their students, and an unwillingness to use the language of authority or power does not change the on-the-ground reality of who is in charge. Freire (1970) made it clear when he said teachers have power over their students, and any suggestion to the contrary is false. Anderson (1987) states that teachers tend to exercise the most power in their domain of control, which is the classroom.

Going a step further, we must understand the reality of choice—or lack of choice—in the relationship. As noted earlier, for the most part, teachers and students do not choose each other. Although there may be instances when parents intervene to choose their child's teacher, the teacher-student relationship generally comes about without either party, especially the student, choosing the other. Therefore, given the teacher's authority and primary job function, the ground rules for interaction tend to be one-sided. Such one-sidedness makes the relationship ripe for power differentials that can be harmful to children, especially the perpetually marginalized, and particularly Black boys.

It cannot be overstated: maintaining order over their primary sphere of control is a lens through which many teachers are viewed as successful. Classroom management is one of the critical components of a teacher's evaluation. Principals want to know their teachers can manage their students. Being able to manage the many personalities and bodies in a classroom is a sign of effectiveness because, as the principal I referred to earlier told me, "If a teacher can't control their kids, they can't teach." Notice here the principal used the language of power: *control*. He did not say, "If a teacher cannot *manage*." He was clear in his use of the word *control* because he wanted to be sure the students were orderly and exhibited what many building leaders expect to see: students seated, silent, and doing what looks like work. We'll revisit this example as one of our case studies. Suffice it to say, adult leadership in the classroom as seen through the ability to manage students is a critical power layer.

The Power Principle

The authority teachers have, which is rooted in a set of knowledge and skills coupled with a law that gives them acting parental rights, forms the basis of what I call the Power Principle. Principles are those rules and structures that govern behavior, and as we move together through this book, you'll be examining the rules and structures that guide how you use the power associated with being an educator.

The Power Principle is all about unpacking how you understand and use the power associated with your authority and responsibility as an educator. It's about fostering a reflective attitude to ensure your understanding and use of power to afford *every* student the opportunity to thrive in your classroom. The Power Principle is about doing some critical self-analysis to more fully understand some of the instructional decisions you make and how those decisions affect students, especially perpetually marginalized students. We all have an ideology about power in our private and professional lives. We may know when to ask for someone with power to act on our behalf, and we're pretty good at knowing when others use their power against us. Unfortunately, as teachers, we've been socialized to believe our role is about benevolence, caretaking, and anything but power. As stated earlier, nothing could be further from the truth. We have power, *and* we use it.

In the United States, the beauty and challenge of not having a national system of education is that every state makes its own determination about how its students will be educated. From funding to staffing to buildings, states set their own policies and procedures. In their autonomy, states give each individual district the ability to make its own governance decisions, and likewise, districts allow building principals to make decisions about how their buildings will operate.

What gets interesting is the degree to which principals pass down autonomy, who they decide should and should not have autonomy, and what type of autonomy they foster. I've worked in many buildings, and they could not be more different. The degree to which I was able to make critical instructional decisions on behalf of my students varied from state to state, district to district, building to building, and, most important, principal to principal. If you're like me, you've paid more attention to principal changes than superintendent changes. I knew each principal had a different perspective on who should govern the instructional decisions for students, and these perspectives would shape how I was expected to approach my teaching. I always waited with bated breath when a new principal was announced because I had to determine the degree to which the instructional autonomy I had come to enjoy would continue or be curtailed. Most times my instructional autonomy continued, and when attempts were made to curtail it, I did what most teachers do: I nodded and waved like the penguins in the movie *Madagascar* ("Smile and wave, boys; just smile and wave"), shut my door, and used my instructional power to help my students learn. In doing so, I was not always correct, and I can even admit to using my instructional power in ways that I'm sure harmed students. It was in reflecting on my own practice and instructional decision making that I came to understand the various ways instructional *autonomy* intersects with the use of instructional *power*.

Instructional power is the undergirding force that moves teaching decisions. Like the previously mentioned "smog in the air" described by Tatum (1997, p. 6), it's something we don't necessarily see, but we know it's there, moving in and through our relationships. But the important point is that we have not stopped to consider it as a force in our decision making. Additionally, we do not stop to consider the beliefs that govern the instructional-power decisions we make. We'll get to those in the next chapter. Right now, we're going to talk about the intersection between instructional autonomy and instructional power.

Instructional autonomy is simply how much freedom or latitude teachers are given to direct the instructional decisions necessary to foster student learning. To a large extent, instructional autonomy is determined by curricular autonomy. Districts purchase and develop curriculum with expectations for how teachers should implement it. You've heard the phrase "implement with fidelity" and recognize the inherent expectation for the curriculum to be followed as the developers designed it, regardless of the degree to which that curriculum meets the unique needs of the students in front of you. In fact, no single curriculum will meet the unique needs of every student across the United States. Curriculum developers know this to be true.

The expectation for curriculum to be implemented with fidelity carries implications for how much freedom teachers will have if they find it necessary to adjust. But purchased curriculum is only part of the instructional decision-making puzzle. Pacing guides and calendars are another. Many districts, especially large districts, have curriculum departments made up of specialists or people holding another title whose job is to determine how the purchased curriculum should be spread across the school calendar year. These calendars provide teachers with a trajectory of student learning designed to cover content, build skills, and ultimately prepare students for statewide assessments. Such calendars sometimes include assessment dates or windows to allow schools flexibility in testing.

In many instances, district-level curriculum specialists are responsible for writing supplemental curriculum and designing learning activities or even writing the district's curriculum with the requisite activities. The expectation about the degree to which teachers follow either the externally purchased or home-grown curriculum can be either in the principal's purview or with someone even further up in the district food chain. Most often, principals determine how curriculum will live in their building.

Instructional autonomy is an essential component of the Power Principle matrix. Let's dive in and explore how the matrix conceptualizes curricular autonomy and other elements that affect your approach to teaching.

The Power Principle Matrix

The Power Principle matrix (Figure 1.1) is a framework for understanding the intersection of your curricular autonomy and your power ideology. It shows the intersections of beliefs, environment,

FIGURE 1.1

The Power Principle Matrix: Levels of Teacher
Autonomy and Dimensions of Instructional Power

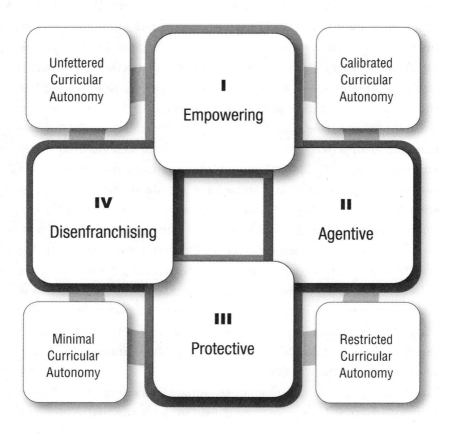

and manifested actions. As a framework, it is important to realize it is not absolute; rather, it is a tool for beginning a process of unpacking and coming to terms with how you approach your teaching, your students' learning, and your classroom environment. It is also a tool for understanding how your ideology affects the students you're privileged to teach.

Research has been very clear about the impact of teachers' ideologies on their student relationships, teaching practice, and student outcomes (CRDC, 2014; Reeves, 2021). Research has been especially clear about the impact of racial/ethnic differences on the outcomes for students of color, especially Black male students, with increasing negative outcomes for Black girls (Morris, 2016). With cultural relevance and sustainability, equity, and educational justice continuing to shape the educational discourse, power dynamics must be part of the discussion, as teachers' decisions have the power to influence the trajectory of students' lives.

The Power Principle matrix has two components—curricular autonomy and power dimensions—representing the core overlapping areas that demonstrate how instructional power operates. We'll begin with unpacking curricular autonomy and then move to the power dimensions.

Levels of Curricular Autonomy

Curricular autonomy is a critical force through which instructional power manifests, which is why I begin unpacking the Power Principle by discussing it. There are countless ways to characterize levels of curricular autonomy. I've chosen four categories to describe degrees of curricular and instructional freedom: Unfettered Curricular Autonomy (UCA), Calibrated Curricular Autonomy (CCA), Minimal Curricular Autonomy (MCA), and Restricted Curricular Autonomy (RCA). As you read each description, think about how the categories relate to the amount of freedom your district and principal allow, keeping in mind you may have experienced different levels at different times in your career.

Unfettered Curricular Autonomy (UCA). If only! This category may be most teachers' dream. In UCA environments, districts and principals give teachers complete control of what, when, and how students learn and how they will be assessed. There is no set curriculum for teachers to follow, and teachers can choose the materials they will use to deliver instruction. Districts or schools tend to focus less on achieving state standards because they tend to have higher-performing students; this critical factor makes school leaders more likely to extend autonomy because less oversight is thought to be needed or required. Because districts or schools with Unfettered Curricular Autonomy allow teachers to make decisions about their teaching materials, resources abound. Teachers have access to a variety of curricular resources from the district and other sources, such as a well-funded parent-teacher association. Strong community relationships and other opportunities make additional resources readily available. Districts or schools in this category tend to be located in wealthy suburbs and cities and are more likely to be less racially and ethnically diverse than others. Additionally, these districts and schools have fewer students experiencing poverty or economic insecurity.

Calibrated Curricular Autonomy (CCA). This category describes the environment that most teachers experience. Districts and schools that allow teachers this level of autonomy may have a focus on standards. The curriculum may be purchased or developed in-house, but teachers have the option to determine the degree to which they will follow it. Much like teachers with UCA, teachers with CCA make decisions about what and how they will teach, but they may not be able to determine when students are assessed, especially at the state level. Teachers may also have freedom to determine formative assessment; however, their summative assessments are likely to be determined by the district. With this level of curricular autonomy, teachers are likely to move against principal and district mandates. Districts or schools in this category are more likely to be well-resourced, with less racial and ethnic diversity and fewer students experiencing poverty or economic instability. Like districts and schools with UCA, those where teachers enjoy Calibrated Curricular Autonomy are resource rich, with community connections such as a parent-teacher association. Students tend to perform well on state-wide assessments, which, as in UCA environments, is a critical factor in decisions to extend the autonomy.

Minimal Curricular Autonomy (MCA). This level of curricular autonomy curtails teachers' curricular decision making. Districts expect adherence to a prescribed curriculum, with little deviation. Deviation—if any—is allowed at the building level. Districts provide pacing guides and calendars, units of study, lessons, and assessments; and teachers make decisions about the degree to which they will follow them only to the extent principals allow. Principals afford curricular autonomy on a case-by-case basis unevenly within their schools. Districts and schools in this category focus heavily on formative and summative assessments. They may be underresourced compared to districts and schools where teachers enjoy UCA and CCA, with many students receiving free or reduced meals. Schools may have limited access to funding sources beyond those provided by the district. These districts and schools also have higher percentages of students of color, multilingual and English language learners, students with disabilities, and students experiencing poverty or economic insecurity.

Restricted Curricular Autonomy (RCA). This category encompasses an environment in which teachers' autonomy is severely constrained. Their districts and schools expect complete adherence to a purchased or in-house curriculum, pacing guides, and lesson plans, and teachers are not allowed to alter the curriculum in any way. Student performance on high-stakes state assessments is a primary focus. Schools are likely to lack resources. The district and schools are likely to be underperforming and contain racially and ethnically marginalized students and students experiencing poverty or economic insecurity. Districts and schools where teachers have RCA are more likely to experience high teacher turnover, which is a critical factor in teachers' lack of autonomy.

What Is Your Teaching Context?

How would you describe your teaching context? Use the following questions as a guide:

- How would you describe the demographics of your school district?
  - Race/ethnicity
  - Economic status
  - Gender
- Does your district perform in line with, above, or below the state on standardized measures?
- How would you describe the curricular involvement of your district?
  - Hands-on: Schools are mandated to follow a set curriculum by grade and content area, with heavy oversight.
  - Detached: Schools are allowed to choose their own curriculum, with little oversight.
  - Mixed bag: Some schools have choice, whereas others do not; the level of oversight depends on the school.
- How would you describe the demographics of the building where you work?
  - Race/ethnicity
  - Economic status
  - Gender
- Does your school perform in line with, above, or below your district and state on standardized measures?
- How would you describe the curricular involvement of the building where you work?
  - Hands-on: Teachers are mandated to follow the district-provided curriculum; no deviation is allowed, and oversight is heavy.

> ○ Detached: Teachers are free to make their own choices with minimal oversight.
> ○ Mixed bag: Freedom and flexibility is a matter of building leaders' discretion, with oversight determined as they see fit.
> • Where do you fit in the curricular involvement of your building?
> • Overall, do your students perform in line with the building, district, and state (if you know this information)?
> • How do your building leaders communicate their curricular expectations to teachers? ▶

Your responses to the reflection questions will give you insight into how curricular autonomy operates in your district and building. It is important to begin here to better understand how it intersects with the Power Principle dimensions discussed in the next section.

Dimensions of Instructional Power

Now that you have a sense of the different types of curricular autonomy and have reflected on your district, building, and personal curricular autonomy, let's examine the instructional power (IP) dimensions. These dimensions are described in terms of the beliefs, environmental factors, and actions teachers take in each category. The dynamism of education means you could be in multiple dimensions at any given time. It's important to realize which dimension you are in, why you may be there, and, if you are in a place where students are being disenfranchised, how to get to a better place for you and your students.

Dimension I/Empowering IP. This dimension is #Goals. As an educator, you want to use your IP to empower students to be full partners in their education so they can use that education to ensure their own well-being outside the school confines. Empowerment goes beyond giving students more and more choice. It is about how students learn the value of the choices they are given the freedom to make. It is about fostering an environment whereby students are in authentic relationships with their peers and their teacher and learn to exercise their agency in ways that do not prevent others from doing the same.

Empowerment is an outcome involving change. It goes beyond students learning a prescribed set of social and emotional skills, having those skills measured, and determining the degrees to which they have "mastered" the self-management competency. Academic subjects become a vehicle of understanding about empowerment and the means through which students develop the decision-making skills to fully enable their abilities to act on their own behalf, for their own well-being—not for the adults' conception of their well-being.

In this environment, students, parents/caregivers, and teachers work collaboratively to understand each other and to ensure students' best interests are centered. Classrooms in the Empowering IP dimension are led by teachers whose ideology is anchored by an unwavering belief that every student is valuable and capable of self-determined decision making. They believe their students possess the rights, skills, and know-how to make sound life choices, even if they don't agree with those choices.

I know—every teacher believes all students can succeed. If only this were true! Research study after research study is clear: not every teacher actually believes *every* student is capable and equally valuable. You may have heard your colleagues talk about students being what Jeff Howard, from the Efficacy Institute, calls "very smart, kinda smart, and kinda dumb" (Raney, 1997). It's not easy to admit, but the common belief that teachers inherently believe in the capability of all students is simply not true. Furthermore, research has been clear about the imbalanced beliefs teachers hold about the abilities of students across racial/ethnic and gender lines. The very fact that a preponderance of teacher development is focused on dispelling deficit ideologies about students of color highlights this unfortunate truth.

What does the Empowering dimension look like in action? Picture a classroom where it is hard to tell the difference between who's teaching and who's learning. Teachers in this dimension actively seek and elevate student voice; they make their students part of not only the learning, but also the planning of the learning. This dimension is an authentic learning partnership born of the belief and ideology that students deserve access to and involvement in the construction of learning. Students are not viewed as empty slates, but rather as people with valuable experiences and knowledge who deserve space to share, learn, and grow. Teachers understand the socializing properties of school and how those properties tend toward disenfranchisement and exclusion, and they actively decode this process with students to champion their success. These teachers help students recognize, understand, and navigate the hidden curriculum. Above all, there is no savior mentality. Children are not viewed as in need of saving because they come from homes the system inherently and implicitly judges as inferior and devalues.

Dimension II/Agentive IP. Think of Dimension II as "I'm getting there." Like their peers in the Empowering dimension, teachers in this dimension hold to the same beliefs about *every* student possessing the skills necessary to succeed academically and in life. They understand learning should be a shared responsibility among teachers, students, and families but may still be reluctant to engage with all families. Classroom educators in this dimension recognize the need for students to have a voice in their learning and are figuring out how to elevate student voice and more authentically bring students into the learning process. They understand agency primarily through the lens of academic choice, whereby students are given options from which to exercise targeted agency; but those choices, although possibly engaging, may not rise to the level of having an influence on students' lives. In the Agentive IP dimension, teachers are the arbiters of the agency students practice, and students may face consequences if they exercise their agency outside what the teachers believe is appropriate. Opportunities for who gets to practice agency may be unevenly distributed. Although teachers are developing their own understanding of agency, they may not have fully come to grips with their underlying biases, which direct who gets to develop and exercise agency and under what school-sanctioned circumstances.

Teachers in this dimension understand how school operates as both a tool and a weapon, particularly with perpetually marginalized students, and they work to help students understand the hidden curriculum of school while also seeking to mitigate the presence of a hidden curriculum within their own classrooms. They understand how school can be culturally violent to groups of students and consider ways to support students.

Perhaps the most critical difference between Empowering IP and Agentive IP is that agentive educators are beginning their journey, whereas their empowering peers are firmly and comfortably down the road on theirs. This distinction is not to suggest that those in the Empowering dimension do not experience hiccups or setbacks; rather, it refers to the teachers' degree of knowledge and practice. Teachers in the Agentive dimension are learning about the critical difference between agency and empowerment because they have realized the need for change and have begun personal learning or have learned from a colleague. They are giving students more say in the running of the classroom and in the assignments and tasks, and they are spending time reflecting on their practices. These teachers are helping students learn about and develop agency skills.

In Dimension II, agency rests at the classroom level, as evidenced by expanded student choice focused on assignments. Students are most likely part of shaping the classroom culture through rule setting and other management structures but may not have opportunities to be involved in the deeper structures of their learning environment, such as lesson planning and grading.

Agentive IP is more widely understood than Empowering IP and often gets confused with its Empowering counterpart. Agency is an element of empowerment in that it involves active decision making, or what Drydyk (2013) refers to as "a given person's degree of involvement in a course of action or to the scope of actions that a person could be involved in bringing about" (p. 251). Sen (1985) more simply explains that "Agency is what a person is free to do and achieve in pursuit of whatever goals or values he or she regards as important" (p. 203). Although both empowerment and agency involve individuals' active participation in and ability to bring about actions on their own behalf, agency does not involve the layer of well-being associated with empowerment. Agency is about the ability to make purposeful choices. A critical difference that distinguishes empowerment is the presence of structures that afford or constrain the development and exercise of decision making. An agentive environment is one where the ability to make one's own decisions is not fully realized due to structural constraints. That is, how the school operates constrains teachers' fostering of students' ability to own their learning. With agency, students are able to make critical choices on their own behalf; however, they are not fully able to control the educative or structural processes that lead to an effective outcome related to life beyond school, as would be the case with empowerment.

Dimension III/Protective IP. When I was supporting a middle school in the Northeast as a coach, I walked into a classroom during the initial visits and was immediately struck by a sign at the teacher's desk that read, "Does This Look Like Your Desk?" This sign sums up Dimension III/Protective IP. In this dimension, protection takes on many forms, the most obvious of which is evidenced by the language around the classroom.

Think of protection as the teacher's need to keep the position of instructional and environmental leader front and center at all times. This is not to be confused with the simplistic notion that teachers and students need clear boundaries; rather, this is about the idea of boundary being weaponized against students to ensure that the teacher's self-identity remains intact. Teachers who operate primarily in the Protective dimension often work hard to demonstrate their ability to tightly manage students. They probably get rewarded for being deemed the best disciplinarians. Although it is true that they have strong classroom management skills, those skills become detrimental to students because the goal is about maintaining the teacher's self-perception more than it is about ensuring a safe and productive learning environment. Dimension III teachers center themselves not as individuals but as members of a group of teachers who strongly believe that teachers are the primary force responsible for students' learning. Students are expected to follow teacher-developed classroom rules, with clearly defined consequences for those who step outside the boundaries. Specific students have voice only to the degree to which the teacher has decided they have earned the right. Student voice is more about students asking questions about their work as opposed to being able to weigh in on the classroom environment or the learning in a meaningful way. There may be the tacit offer "Let's make classroom rules together" that allows students to add items to an already prepared list of do's and don'ts; but such involvement does not rise to the level of authentic coconstruction, where teacher and students develop a way of being in the classroom.

Dimension III educators may actually be viewed quite positively by administrators and colleagues because they get results in the traditional way results are viewed. Their students may perform well on high-stakes assessments, their classrooms are orderly—even quiet—and students appear to be successful. But kick the tires or look under the hood and you'll likely find troubling signs that will make you question the veneer of success.

In this environment, students must adhere to strict codes of behavior, such as only speaking when spoken to by the teacher or having to get permission to engage with a classmate. Rules govern how to access classroom materials, with consequences if the rules are not followed. Teachers in this environment use language in ways that, upon examination, are quite cringeworthy, as in the following example.

My travels to a school in the South led me to a middle school ELA classroom led by a teacher I'll call Amy, where students were allowed to check books out of the classroom library. The procedure for students to check out the book was for them to write their name and sign-out date on a list, and, upon completing the book, sign the book back in by writing the return date on the list next to their name. The last step had to be done *before* the book was put back on the shelf. Sounds good, right? Procedures are necessary to keep track of limited supplies, and students must learn how to be responsible and held accountable to ensure every student has the opportunity to enjoy books. Well, a student I'll call Jake followed Part A of the procedure; he chose a book and wrote his name and the check-out date on the form, as required. During my visit, Jake was eager to get to work, and he put the book back on the shelf without following Part B of the procedure: he neglected to write the return date. What I witnessed was horrifying. As students completed their independent work, Amy walked the aisle checking on their progress while also checking the book-list form on a clipboard. Here's the exchange:

> Amy: Jake, where's the book?
>
> Jake: It's on the shelf.
>
> Amy: I don't see the return date on the form, so the book's not back.
>
> Jake: Look at the first book on the shelf. I been turn't that in. I forgot to write the date down.
>
> Amy: You were supposed to write the date on the list to check it back in before putting it back on the shelf. . . . And it's "I turned it in already," not "I been turn't." . . . Please say it correctly.
>
> Jake: I turned it in already. The book is on the shelf; it's the first book on that row. Go look. I returned it.
>
> Amy: You didn't write the return date on the form, so you didn't return the book.

Jake: The book is right on the shelf. I just forgot to write the date, but it's on the shelf. Just go look.

Amy: I'm not going to look because you *know* you're supposed to write the return date *before* you put the book back. So until *you* write the return date, the book is still considered out.

Jake: I just forgot. [sigh]

Amy: Well, next time you *won't* forget 'cause you're not taking another book until this is done the way I explained.

Now, we can argue about the need for the student to follow the procedure; however, the teacher's need to engage the student in a discussion about the book-return policy when the book was clearly where the child put it demonstrates the teacher's need to protect her rules under the guise of making classroom supplies readily available to all students. This teacher also had a need to teach the student a lesson about the necessity of adhering to policies simply for the sake of adhering to policies. A simple reminder about the procedure would have sufficed; instead, a student's opportunity to enjoy books was revoked because in his rush to start his classwork to avoid other infractions, he forgot to write a date on a line. If I lost an opportunity every time I forgot something . . . well, I'm confident my life would be quite different than it is now, and I'm sure yours would be, too.

Consider this second example, involving my observation of a 7th grade teacher in the Northeast. Her principal was excited for me to spend time with her because he found her to be especially skilled in classroom management. During my observation, I agreed with the principal's assessment. This teacher's classroom appeared to run like a well-oiled machine. Students moved through the beginning portion of the lesson with ease, knowing exactly what to do, how to interact with their peers, and how to turn in their assignment. When the "Do Now" portion of the lesson was completed, the teacher began the lesson with a reminder of the learning objectives. Although students had appeared independent during the "Do Now," the environment changed during the lesson's core aspects. Students received a worksheet they were to complete based on the information the teacher provided. The document contained five sentences, which the teacher read out loud. When it was time for students to fill in the blank, the teacher stopped and said, "This is the information you need from me." She then proceeded to spell the word students needed. I observed a student moving ahead to complete the worksheet, and when the teacher noticed this, she stopped the class and said to the student, "You know that's not how we do things here. You are to wait for me until I say it's time to move to the next sentence." The child stopped working and waited for the teacher.

During our debrief, I asked the teacher why she wanted students to wait for her instead of allowing them the independence she had afforded them during the "Do Now" work. She explained that the "Do Now" was simply a review of work from a previous lesson, and she knew her students would not need her help; she was confident about their skills in the "Do Now." She then explained that during the lesson, it was important for students to follow her because they were below grade level and could advance better when she told them the information. Finally, she explained that her students needed to have precise information to complete their work because if she did not give them the information, they would put the wrong answers on their pages and they would not do well on tests given later.

This teacher is clearly adept at saying what most teachers believe about education while protecting their space and beliefs about their own intellectual superiority and hiding their underlying beliefs about their students' capacity, masking those beliefs as concern for their students' need for more emphasis on nonacademics. It is important not to misplace your compassion because you believe students' life circumstances are the reason they are unable to do high-level academic work.

Protective IP is the most challenging dimension to detect. The actions are subtle and require educators to have a keen understanding of how teachers' language can unintentionally reveal what they may be working to protect. Most often they are protecting their position and belief systems, many of which, if articulated, would be offensive. These are the teachers who have yet to fully acknowledge the inherent racism in the school system and are in denial about teacher bias, including—and especially—their own. These are the teachers most likely to say, "I treat all students the same" or the dreaded "I don't see color. I see my students as people." Later, we'll talk more about why these statements are inaccurate and, more important, dangerous to the learning environment. For now, the point to remember is the presence of an underlying belief that adults know best, and any choices students get should be within the confines of what the teacher decides to be useful for academic learning.

Dimension IV/Disenfranchising IP. If you've ever written a rubric, you know the highest and lowest evaluation descriptors are the easiest to spot. You definitely know what "exceeds" and "does not meet" look like. Such is the case with these dimensions of instructional power. Dimension I/Empowering IP is easier to spot than, say, Dimension III/Protective IP. However, Dimension IV, although among the easiest to spot, is the most troubling to encounter. In my view, only one word describes teachers who operate with Disenfranchising IP: *toxic*. I'm sure there are other applicable words, and after reading this description, feel free to substitute your own.

Teachers who demonstrate Disenfranchising IP believe students, especially young children, are blank slates, and it is the teacher's responsibility to fill their brains with everything they need to be successful in school. Teachers in Dimension IV have a clear deficit mentality about students who are racially, ethnically, and especially economically and linguistically different from them. They see difference as deficit. Although this deficit thinking may be evident in Dimension III and may linger in Dimension II, it is clear and pervasive with teachers in Dimension IV. Their belief systems are evident in the use of language such as "these kids," "those children," and the unthinkable but heard from the mouth of a teacher, "the natives are restless." The use of "these" and "those" to name student groups is usually followed by statements about the students' abilities, perceived family background, use of speech, how they dress, or any other way of being that sits outside what the teacher values or believes is appropriate for school.

In addition to evidencing their deficit thinking, teachers in this dimension use the structures of school as a weapon of control. There is no collaborating on classroom rules. Rules have been established, and students face escalating consequences when they step outside the line. Again, this situation may not feel different than, say, what would happen if students break the rules in an Agentive IP classroom; however, the critical difference here is that Disenfranchising IP teachers will use punishment as their first response, whereas those in the Empowering or Agentive dimensions will use punishment as a last resort or not at all. Disenfranchising classrooms are adult-centered, and the students are the mechanism through which teachers get to demonstrate their knowledge and their ability to control children— and ultimately to get a paycheck.

Disenfranchising teachers are protective of both their position and their physical space; they are overtly biased against their students in terms of factors including race, gender, and language; and where there is express knowledge of a student's economic situation, these teachers will use such knowledge to lower standards and accept inferior work to prove that economics is the reason a student underperforms. In Disenfranchising IP classrooms, students who speak devalued varieties of English experience academic ridicule disguised as preparing students for the real world, and their speech is corrected even when they are not engaged in academic work. Disenfranchising IP teachers use sarcasm as a way to appear funny and hip (I know, I'm dating myself with that word) and don't care about how the sarcasm lands in students' ears—but more important, in students' hearts.

In Disenfranchising IP classrooms, the teachers have structured the rules, and there is no mistaking who's in charge. In the actual words of a teacher, "They know this is my classroom, and they will not overtake me." Students know exactly where their relational boundaries lie. There is something good to be said about knowing one's boundaries; however, the situation is altogether different when those boundaries are exclusionary and adversarial and create an atmosphere where students get the message that they do not belong.

The Dimension IV classroom is a weapon against children, with teachers using all their tools to control students' thinking and movement. From assignments, to grading, to when children are allowed to speak or not speak, to how they are allowed to express their understanding of content, this classroom and the teacher who leads it are anti-children. Like their Dimension III/Protective counterparts, these teachers may be heralded as proficient because they have what are considered strong management skills, and many of their students may perform well on high-stakes tests; however, upon deeper examination, these teachers are bullying students (Reed Marshall, 2016). They know their power, and instead of using it to foster agentive development or move toward empowerment, they protect themselves and disenfranchise students. They manage by threat. At lower grade levels, threat takes the form of possibly losing recess or having silent lunch, having a valued classroom job taken away, or something more subtle but no less damaging, such as purposefully mispronouncing a student's name or asking about clothing or hair. In the upper grades, threat may take the form of being assigned more work—especially work piled on top of existing assignments to prove course rigor; grading irregularities, which demonstrate clear favoritism; and disciplinary action such as sending students to colleagues for minor offenses—the same offenses for which other students receive only warnings or no response at all.

Finally (and I can imagine you asking yourself, *There's more?*), disenfranchising teachers hold students accountable against a hidden curriculum that sees school as a reproductive agent for society. Unlike their empowering or agentive counterparts, disenfranchising teachers are ill-equipped or unwilling to recognize this element of their praxis; therefore, this may be the only subconscious aspect of their behavior. They simply understand schooling as the primary tool through which students learn about society and see their role as instrumental in making sure students learn and adhere to societal rules as advanced in school.

Certainly, students must learn how society works, but doing so must *never* be at the expense of their sense of self. Students should not have to shelve their identities to be successful in school; and in the disenfranchising classroom, as in the protective classroom, students—especially those who do not fit a dominant cultural framework—are expected to do just that in order to be successful both academically and socially.

II PAUSE TO REFLECT

What Is Your Understanding of Power?

How do you understand power? Answer the following questions to unpack how you think about instructional power:

- How do you describe power?
- Do you consider yourself as having power?
- Do you consider yourself to be in charge of your classroom?
- How often do you partner with students to set classroom procedures?
  - Always
  - Often
  - Sometimes
  - Never
- Why might you have different processes for establishing classroom rules for different classes?

- When student behavior must be redirected, do you see it as a need to control or a need to manage?
- How often do you reflect on the decisions you make regarding your instructional practices?
  - Always
  - Often
  - Sometimes
  - Never
- Is there a class or classes where you have noticed students engaging in what would be a challenge to your authority (i.e., pushing your buttons)?
  - If so, when is this most likely to occur?
  - If so, are there students who do this more than others?
  - If so, how are you most likely to respond?
- Is there a class or classes where you have noticed students engaging in what would be considered peer-to-peer power struggles?
  - If so, how has this affected your classroom environment?
  - If so, how do you most often respond? ▶

Your responses to the reflection questions reveal how you think about power and whether you notice possible power dynamics in your classroom. Your responses also provide insight into how you address potential power struggles.

Looking Ahead

In the coming chapters, I will break down aspects of the matrix to help you see how it operates and suggest ways you can shift your practice to become more aware of how you use your instructional power. The intent is to support you as you make the choice to move forward toward building authentic agency and empowerment.

2 | THE POWER PRINCIPLE AND TEACHER BELIEFS

I believe every student can learn.

As noted earlier, this declaration is perhaps one of the most familiar statements teachers make. It expresses an inherent belief in students' abilities; however, it's the "every student" part that we'll now analyze through the Power Principle matrix to see how what we say does not always align with what we really believe, which gets manifested through our actions.

So what is belief? The dictionary tells us *belief* is a noun, which means it's a *thing*, and this thing is the acceptance of some other thing as true. A belief is also a statement of confidence and trust in someone, and in the case of teachers, the expressed belief is that all students can learn. However, as we know, research has demonstrated a clear and even widening gap between what teachers say they believe about students and what they actually believe.

In their 2018 study titled "The Opportunity Myth," The New Teacher Project (TNTP) asked teachers whether they believed students could be successful in achieving high academic standards. Of the more than one thousand teachers surveyed, 82 percent said yes. That is, 82 percent believed all students could reach high-rigor standards. Unfortunately, in the same group, only 44 percent believed the students they actually taught could handle the rigor of high academic standards. That gap is nearly a 50 percent drop in belief or confidence in students.

What caused this dramatic difference? Among myriad possible reasons, one of the most prevalent is teachers' perceptions about students from various racial and ethnic backgrounds and how those perceptions influence their ideologies and expectations about the intellectual capacity of these students. Findings from this same study revealed stark disparities in the rigor of work students from various racial and ethnic groups received. If you are being honest with yourself, you probably have some idea about which groups of students received which types of assignments. Unfortunately, predictive analytics supports the assumptions you are most likely making. Black and Hispanic/Latinx students received the least rigorous assignments regardless of the class they were in, and Asian/Asian American and White students received the most rigorous assignments regardless of the level of their class. Such belief disparities require some unpacking.

Looking at History

To understand this gap between belief and action, especially as it relates to Black students, we have to walk through a bit of history. From the founding days of the United States, only those who descended from European populations were considered human and valued as such. All other groups, especially those enslaved and brought here against their will, were considered subhuman and deserving of subjugation. The notion that Black people were incapable of human actions such as thinking and feeling justified enslavement and permeated every aspect of American life. Learning was withheld from enslaved Africans and African Americans, and those who dared to become literate did so under the threat of being brutalized, sold, and murdered. Those caught teaching an enslaved person to read, write, or use numbers faced similar risk unless they were White, in which cases their punishment was less severe (Williams, 2005). To White enslavers, learning was unnecessary and dangerous for Black people because, as Frederick Douglass's slaveholder stated, "a literate slave was a dangerous slave" (Williams, 2005, p. 25). Being able to read meant the enslaved could understand and challenge the moral incongruence of America fighting for its freedom while simultaneously working to hold humans as captives. Along with the belief in literacy being dangerous, the prevailing science of the time contended that Africans, based on their skull size and configuration, were inherently less intellectually capable than White people (Gould, 1981). These ideologies shaped the overarching and underlying beliefs about who could learn and who could not learn.

To maintain this belief system, rooted in white supremacist ideology—which is the system and structure built around the ideas that White people are more intelligent, more capable, and thus more deserving—laws were enacted to ensure the separation of people by race. The Plessy v. Ferguson Supreme Court ruling of 1890 held that, indeed, Black and White people were different and should be separated; as long as places of business, education, and other institutions were "equal," separation was to be the law.

Although "separate but equal" was the *law*, it was not the *way*. Despite evidence of Black and White students attending mixed-race schools, Plessy v. Ferguson made it unlawful for this mixing to occur on a large scale. Furthermore, "separate but equal" was anything but equal, and it took another ruling to undo this structure. "Separate but equal schooling" was a misnomer, as Black children were forced to accept underfunded schools, limited academic resources, and restricted school programming. (Wait—am I talking about the 19th century? This sounds so much like schools in the 21st century!)

Fast forward. We're all familiar with the landmark 1954 case Brown v. Board of Education of Topeka, which made the institution of "separate but equal" unconstitutional and ushered in the largest education reform in U.S. history. Once the Supreme Court signed Brown into law and states began to enact it, the educational ground upon which Black students stood shook dramatically. The Brown decision changed the landscape of education in the United States as Black students came face-to-face with people who had lived their lives believing in the intellectual inferiority of an entire race. These people were now charged with educating a group of students they did not believe was capable of learning.

History is replete with desegregation narratives of Black students having to be ushered into "White" schools by armed guards, only to be met by teachers who were vocal in their disdain for their presence. You may have even shared the story of Ruby Bridges with your students—and if you have not, I would encourage you to do so. Ruby Bridges spent her entire 1st grade year in a classroom by herself because her Louisiana school would not allow White students to learn alongside her. When the results of the school's equivalent to end-of-year summative assessments came out and Ruby's scores were higher than those of many White students, her abilities were questioned, and she was accused of somehow cheating. It was unthinkable that a Black child would be on par with—let alone exceed—a White child on an academic assessment.

Although Ruby's experiences might seem like they occurred a long time ago, consider this: she was born the same year the Brown legislation was signed—1954. You probably have family members the same age as Ruby; I certainly do. The year 2019 marked the 65th anniversary of the signing of this remarkable document. It was not that long ago; yet teachers are still holding on to disparate systems of belief about who can and who cannot succeed, about who has the intellectual abilities to handle rigorous standards and coursework and who does not.

This discussion matters because we have to see the present through the eyes of the past. As educators, we are all about fixing situations; however, if past is considered prologue, then we have to take time to better understand our past so the prologue can be interrupted. We are all about action; however, unexamined contexts ensure a repeat of past errors. The United States speaks of liberty and justice for all; however, the underlying ideology of White people being better, smarter, and more deserving continues to permeate its structures. Now you may ask, "Well, there are racialized groups who outperform White students in schools; isn't that something to dispel the myth of white exceptionalism?" Glad you asked. The answer is no. We hold fast to constructs about groups of people to fit neatly into our belief systems and box people in to make what we believe true.

In thinking about the relationship between our beliefs and our actions, it is imperative to understand the cultural dynamics of the classroom to see where the breakdown occurs. Classrooms are cultural exchange sites. Culture takes shape the instant teachers meet students and students meet one another. From their first encounters, the tone is set, rules are laid down, and the operational functions of the classroom take shape.

When public schooling began in the United States, people gave little thought to the cultural dynamics of the classroom. The culture was built on a set of principles based on Judeo-Christian ideals, with clearly defined roles for teachers and students. As the United States became multicultural and multiracial, schooling remained fixed on old principles about how people should relate to one another. Classrooms reflect society's norms; however, such norms have left and continue to leave many people in a state of perpetual marginalization. Additionally, little or no consideration is given to the customs and practices of different racial and ethnic groups, how girls may learn in ways that are different from how boys learn, or any other norm outside the patriarchal understandings of White males. Although schools have most certainly made progress (Seneca Keyes, 2019), much remains to do until all students know they belong in the classes where they have been placed.

The Cultured Classroom

School is society's teacher. It is the place where kids go to learn how to be good citizens. They learn how to be in society by learning the rules, how to follow them, and what happens if they do not follow them. A tacit understanding tells us that school will be the primary vehicle through which students will acquire the necessary skills to become productive members of society.

Here's the challenge: our unresolved history related to citizenship becomes the filter through which teachers make decisions about who fits into the culture of their classroom and who does not. Such ideologies lie under the surface and can be unconscious yet are visible to students because actions speak louder than any spoken word. Go back to the opening sentence in this chapter: "I believe every student can learn." Those words come out of the mouths of thousands of teachers every day, yet the results of the 2018 TNTP study reveal a different reality.

What cultural norms are students meant to acquire that will relegate those who do not follow them to the classroom margins? How do students learn about whether they fit or not? How does power shape the expression of who fits and who does not fit? These are questions teachers ask me all the time. And although the gap between belief and action regarding everyone's ability to learn is concerning, I am hopeful that the ideas presented here will push people to consider their lenses and filters and force them to reconsider how they understand the structure of their instructional practices.

Culture is messy and not easily defined. Ask teachers to describe the culture of their classroom and they are likely to ask you, "Which class?" because each has a different culture. The issue of whether certain groups of students "fit" is not related to whether teachers decide to keep students in rows or put them in communal circles; it is related to how teachers communicate their belief systems through their interactions.

I conducted a case study with a group of teachers to understand how they connected their understanding of culture to their understanding of how power intersects with their belief systems and instructional decision making. Each one explained culture in a different way. The educator who stood out the most was one I named Beth, who defined culture as the "beliefs, attitudes, practices of a particular place or group of people." By beginning her definition with *beliefs*, Beth signaled the significance of one's beliefs on the other ideas that followed. As she spoke more about her classroom, she made it clear that each of her classes was unique, and the human interactions shaped the culture of each one differently. In thinking about the particularity of place coupled with the beliefs of those involved, we can clearly see how power can influence the cultural dynamics of a classroom. Another participant centered her definition of culture around the contributions of those in a particular environment; and another likened culture to nesting dolls, with each aspect of an individual fitting inside other aspects and combining with other nesting dolls to create an environment where the cultural dynamic is an amalgamation of nested people.

Teachers are the primary leaders in shaping the classroom cultural dynamic because the classroom is their area of control. In formulating the structures to ensure a safe and orderly learning environment, teachers institute processes and procedures that reflect what they believe is necessary to create the type of space conducive to maximum learning. The degree to which all those nested individuals—the students—find space for expression rests with a teacher whose beliefs, attitudes, and practices lie at the center.

‖ PAUSE TO REFLECT

What Factors Shape Your Classroom Culture?

To make your work with the Power Principle matrix more effective, it's time to examine your classroom culture by reflecting on your beliefs, attitudes, and practices. You need to think critically about how these factors are shaping the culture of the classroom. This reflective exercise begins with a brief look into a mirror—*your mirror*—to identify basic personal attributes. It then moves to a walk down memory lane as you reflect on your early schooling. Finally, it prompts you to reflect on your current professional setting.

As you respond to the questions in each section, resist the urge to sugarcoat yourself because some of the questions are difficult or uncomfortable to answer. You and your students deserve honest responses.

Looking into Your Mirror

Describe the basic elements of your identity by answering the following four-part question:

- How do you identify in terms of the following characteristics?
  - Race
  - Ethnicity
  - Gender
  - Economic status

Walking Down Memory Lane

Choose an early memory about your own schooling. As you work through the questions, remember: try not to sugarcoat your responses.

- Describe the culture of the school you are remembering.
- Describe the culture of the neighborhood where this school was located.

- What did your school value?
  - How were values communicated?
  - How did the school values align with your family or neighborhood values?
  - How did community members interact with one another?
  - Were teachers from the neighborhood?
- Describe the culture of the school.
  - How did the adults help you learn about the culture of the school?
  - Were all the cultures in the school equally accepted and respected?
  - Were there cultures more accepted and respected than others? Which ones?
  - Were there cultures less accepted and respected than others? Which ones?
  - How were you able to determine which cultural norms were more or less accepted and respected than others?
- Were you part of a group that was more accepted/respected or less accepted/respected?
  - If you were part of a group that was more accepted and respected, how was this communicated to you?
  - If you were part of a group that was less accepted and respected, how was this communicated to you?
  - Were you aware of differences in how groups of students were treated?
  - How did the adults in your class or building communicate to you that you belonged or did not belong?
- Name a specific time when you felt most accepted and respected in school.
  - What were the specific actions the adults used to foster this feeling?
  - How were words used to communicate this sense of acceptance and respect?

- Name a specific time when you felt least accepted or less respected in school.
  - What were the specific actions the adults used to foster this feeling?
  - How were words used to communicate this lack of acceptance or lack of respect?
- What do you think contributed to how the adults interacted with you to communicate a sense or lack of belonging? Did you feel as though your acceptance was based on factors beyond your control (e.g., your gender, race, family connections)?

Examining the Present

As you address the questions in the following section, you will read about two educators, Erin and Beth, whose experiences will help you understand the implications of culture, beliefs, and community connectedness on instructional decision making.

- Describe the culture of the school or building where you currently work.

  Erin and Beth worked at the same high school, where the culture can best be described as male-dominant and sports-focused, with female students and teachers viewed as being props to ensure the male students involved in sports were supported. Male students were privileged above female students, and students involved in sports and those in advanced courses were privileged above all other students. The building leader had been a football coach and winner of state championships.

- Describe the culture of the neighborhood where the school is located.

  The culture of the neighborhood where Beth and Erin worked was shaped by a sense of Southern rural closeness. Many of the school employees had grown up in the town, which gave them an insiders' knowledge about the students, as their lives crossed paths outside school. Many of the adults had personal connections to students beyond school because of the smallness of the town and their having grown up in the community. Erin had been the babysitter to one of her students.

- Are the teachers from the neighborhood where the school is located?

  Erin and several other teachers were from the neighborhood; Beth was from the state, but not from the neighborhood.

- What does your school value?
  - How are those values communicated?
  - Do those values align to the community values?
  - Do those values align to your personal values?
- What do you value in your class?
  - How do you communicate those values?
  - Is there complete alignment between the values expressed and lived out in your classroom and those expressed and lived in your school or building?
- Describe the culture of your class. (Middle or high school teachers should choose one class to describe.)
  - How was the culture of your class established?
  - How does the culture reflect your values?
  - Are you a member of the community where you teach? If not, how does the community where you live compare to the community where you teach?
  - How do the differences between your home community and the school community influence your thoughts, speech, and actions with your students? (You must be honest about how you think about your students, especially if their community differs from yours along racial/ethnic and economic lines.)
  - Do your students know what you value?
  - How did they learn about your values?
  - What do your students value?
  - How did you learn about their values?

○ How do your values and their values align?
○ What are the differences between what you and your students value?

For Beth, the classroom reflected African American culture, as the student population was more than 90 percent African American. According to Beth, this culture was most prevalent in students' linguistic exchanges, including a common practice of playing the dozens, in which students banter with one another in ways that could be considered insulting. To an untrained ear, playing the dozens can be off-putting; however, to one who understands it, playing the dozens is a linguistic art form. According to Beth, many of the students had grown up in the town and knew each other fairly well, creating a classroom with an air of familiarity and familial closeness. For Erin, who had attended this school, her classroom culture could be described as a family. Her students, like Beth's, engaged in the dozens—and so did she. Beth was familiar with her students, as she had known many of them outside school. She and her students shared many of the same values and ways of speaking and interacting.

○ Where was there tension between your culture and your students' culture in establishing the overall culture of your class, and how were these tensions resolved?

As an outsider, Beth felt tension in the cultural differences between her students and herself. It is important to note the tension stemmed more from cultural differences—primarily in students playing the dozens—than racial differences. Beth did not fully understand the practice and admitted to treating it initially as a form of bullying, which led her to respond by sending students to the office only to have them sent back with no disciplinary action being taken. She did not understand why students would insult one another in ways she believed were harmful to their relationships. Beth's family did not play the dozens; she had no experience with the practice, and her students engaging in it at inopportune times during the learning cycle caused tension. Her natural teacher response was to refer students—until she chose to learn about the practice from her students and allow them to use it during agreed-upon times and in ways that would not disrupt learning and extend beyond boundaries she and her students established.

○ Is there a predominant culture governing the interactions, established rules, and discipline structures of your class?

For Beth, a predominant culture governing the interactions of her class caused her to struggle to connect with her students and at times made teaching a challenge. Language was the driving force of how culture emanated from students. Her students' use of language differed greatly from her own, and she neither understood it nor believed it should have a place in her classroom. She recalled times when certain students would be disinterested in the lesson and begin playing the dozens, which would throw off her lesson. Because the students who began the game were highly respected among their peers, she found it difficult to challenge their use of language in trying to get them back on track for learning. Beth made it clear that many of the students who initiated the game were her most successful academically, which created an even bigger challenge because they were still able to complete their work. Eventually, rather than use what she called strong-arm tactics such as sending students to the office or removing them from class, Beth chose to let them play the dozens when she felt it wouldn't take up too much class time. ▸

Your responses to these questions are critical in understanding how your class operates. It is imperative to take a deep look into the dynamics governing your interactions with your students and their interactions with each other. How culture gets established is a matter often taken for granted, as though it simply happens; however, the questions you just considered are crucial in thinking about how you, as the power center of the class, shape and direct the cultural flow. Your students are an amalgamation of personalities, cultures, ideologies, genders, races, and ethnicities that must be brought together to ensure learning. You must find a way to create a cohesive community whereby each person is known and valued, and they *know* that you know and value them.

Now let's step off the happy train here and admit that we do not like every student equally. We gravitate to some students more easily than others. However, we cannot lean so heavily into our personal preferences for behaviors, personalities, cultures, races, genders, and other elements that we signal exclusion to the students we deem difficult. We have to use metacognition—thinking about our thinking—to help disrupt those thoughts that lead to the behaviors that create disenfranchising learning environments for many of our students.

Power and Beliefs

As we discussed in Chapter 1, power is the ever-present force woven through every relationship and most interactions. The need to navigate power dynamics is a constant. Children begin this process at a very young age—just ask the parent of the average 2-year-old who has just learned the word *no* and understands the possibility of *not* doing something, such as eating dinner. Even at that young age, children are learning how to negotiate their power and that of others. The classroom is exactly the same. Young people are learning how to negotiate and navigate the dynamics of power, though many of them have never considered the possibility that they possess the right to do so. Others, of course, are fully aware of their ability to exercise their agency and will do so on a regular basis—sometimes positively and other times, not so much. Students whose families engage in discussions about power will have a better understanding of it versus those whose families do not.

II PAUSE TO REFLECT

What Influence Did Your Family Have on Your Beliefs About Power?

Consider your own upbringing as you answer these questions:
- Was there a clear line of authority in your family?
  - Who was in charge?
  - How were children expected to behave toward the person(s) in charge?
- Did your family have discussions about power?
- Were you (and your siblings, if you had any) allowed to voice your own thoughts or opinions, or were you expected to adopt your parents'/caregivers' line of thinking?
  - If you were not allowed to voice a dissenting thought or opinion, what were the consequences when you (or your siblings) did so? ▶

Your answers to the reflection questions form the lenses through which you view students and their natural tendency to want space to develop their own thoughts and opinions. If you grew up in a household with clear lines of authoritative demarcation, you might find it difficult when students push back and ask questions about their work, your teaching, or ideas you think they should hold. On the other hand, growing up in such an environment just might make you more open to and understanding of students who want to practice their agency. If you grew up in a household where your voice was sought and allowed to be exercised, such actions may not be as much of a challenge for you (unless you believed such freedom was wrong as you were growing up). Just like adults, children have various dispositions, and the intersection of their nature and their environment (nurture) affects the degree to which they will be more or less likely to exercise their agency toward becoming a fully empowered person. As the adult, you have to understand your lens and how it affects the way you interact with your students and the responses you have to their need to develop agency. This understanding is especially important for secondary teachers. The very nature of adolescents is to work toward independence from the adults in their lives. Their development requires that they learn how to navigate the power waters around them. The degree to which you understand your belief systems about power is the degree to which you will aid or hinder your students' growth in this area.

Not only must you more fully understand your ideologies, which get manifested in your beliefs and actions; you also have to be especially honest about how you process race and ethnicity. How you process these factors from a value perspective is essential to uncovering how you will handle students from various races and ethnic backgrounds. Before you go off into the ever-popular, grossly erroneous, and problematic "I don't see color; I only see people," I will stop you and say if that was your first reaction, you already have an issue. To not see the physical body of a student is to *not see the student*. Unwillingness to say you recognize that you have students from a variety of backgrounds, which includes their race and ethnicity, is requiring your students to shelve their identities and conform to a universalized identity, which most often means you will be requiring your students who are not White to be White in their actions and speech. Research has been clear: people begin to recognize race at very early ages (Aboud, 2008).

I remember the first time a White colleague told me she did not see color. I asked her why. She looked at me stunned, as if to question why I would even think to push her on that response and said she saw me as a beautiful person. I went a step further and asked her if she thought her clothes matched that day, to which she giggled and responded yes. My response to her and others who tell me they don't see color was "If your clothes match, you see color." The issue is not whether you recognize the various skin complexions people have; it's what happens inside your brain when you recognize the variations.

As teachers, although we seldom declare ourselves to be powerful, we are among the most significant adults in a young person's life. Our power must be understood in relation to the ideologies and beliefs we hold. We must realize that what we believe shapes our decisions, and power is the force we use to enact our ideological systems upon children. Beliefs have been encoded and reinforced in multiple ways.

Having posed a series of general questions around your family, we are going to turn now to questions about how you learned about race. These questions are necessary to help you gain a deeper understanding about the intersections of the belief structures you hold.

ǀǀ PAUSE TO REFLECT

How Did You Learn About Race?

As with all reflection questions, be honest in your responses to these questions about your upbringing. You and your students need you to be.

- When did you learn about race or racism?
- If you identify as White, when did you realize being White was different than being another race?
- If you identify as a person of color, when did you realize you were that race?

- Did your family talk about race or racism?
  - If so, how did they build understanding about different races?
  - If so, how did they build understanding about racism?
- If your family did not openly discuss race or racism, how did they talk about other races/ethnicities?
  - How did hearing your parents/caregivers, siblings, and other family members talk about different races influence your beliefs about different races?
- Have your beliefs and understanding about different races and racism changed in your adult life?
- Think about the race with which you most identify. How do you view your identified race in relation to the dominant culture of U.S. society?
- How does your identification and relationship to other races shape your interactions with your students? ▶

As you did with the previous sets of questions, be sure to consider how your answers may be shaping how you approach your instructional decision making and interactions with students. These considerations make up your ideologies about race and racism. They become the lenses through which you see and interact with students.

Beliefs and the Matrix

Although we may not be able to control the amount of curricular autonomy we have in our districts and buildings, we can control how we use our power with our students. Decision-making power is only part of the power dynamic. The other part relates to how the classroom culture and environment are created. It reveals itself in the subtle messages teachers send students through their actions and words, and through the actions and words allowed between students. Students have a much keener eye than adults give them credit for. Even the students who benefit from the power imbalance recognize that benefit and play the game to their advantage and often to that of their friends.

As discussed in Chapter 1, the intersectionality between curricular autonomy and the dimensions of instructional power shapes the overall learning environment. It would be easy to assume that teaching in a setting governed by Restricted Curricular Autonomy equals a Dimension III/Protective or Dimension IV/Disenfranchising environment and teaching in a setting with Unfettered Curricular Autonomy means teachers automatically enact Dimension I/Empowering and Dimension II/Agentive as their power domain. Nothing could be further from the truth. Curricular autonomy is an avenue through which the power dimensions are evidenced as teachers work to support student learning. One type of curricular autonomy does not automatically equate to a particular power-dimensional counterpart.

Because all learning is relational and transactional, the imbalances in authoritative power show up through instructional decisions made in relation to the amount of curricular autonomy *and* within the relationships developed between teachers and students and between students and their peers outside the instructional space. Teacher belief systems drive the use of instructional power in conjunction with curricular autonomy.

Consider a case involving a teacher I'll call Dawn, who taught in a well-resourced high school in the Northeast. I conducted several observations in her AP English classroom, where she had Unfettered Curricular Autonomy and students were headed to colleges across the country, including Ivy League colleges. Dawn's class had all the appearances of Dimension I/Empowering instructional power. Her classroom library was enviable. Students sat at round tables to encourage dialogue and moved easily about the classroom. The building atmosphere was much the same. Students moved about without adult supervision; they could choose from among carefully designed gathering spaces to have lunch or meet with peers, or they could eat in the hallways. This was the type of school any parents would want their child to attend.

I visited Dawn's classroom several times and noticed something quite interesting. There were no set rules for how students used language. They were allowed to demonstrate knowledge using the words they felt best conveyed their understanding. Dawn spent no time correcting students and used colloquialisms as deftly as her students did. Language was a tool for expression, not a weapon in the way Amy, whom you met in Chapter 1, used it.

On an upcoming project, students were to work with a peer of their choice to analyze two books from the classroom library. The project directions gave students specific guidance about how they should approach their reading. One of the pairs of books was *Purple Hibiscus*, by Chimamanda Ngozi Adiche, and *Things Fall Apart*, by Chinua Achebe. Students were directed to think about the impact of colonization, and Dawn typed into the project form, "I strongly suggest you read *Things Fall Apart* first." For another pairing—*Just Mercy*, by Bryan Stevenson, and *To Kill a Mockingbird*, by Harper Lee—students were directed to think about justice, injustice, and the role race plays in justice. Suggestions such as these were in place for all eight pairings. Students were told, "You may want to think about . . . ," with Dawn providing the topics she believed should guide their reading and analytical focus.

As we got to know each other, Dawn said she did not necessarily believe in teachers having power—that is, if teachers were holding power over their students, the students would not be able to learn. Ideologically, Dawn believed students should be able to choose what they read and get from their reading what they need. Her students had access to an extensive library from which they could choose books. There were no rules about how long a book could be borrowed or how many books could be borrowed at any given time. Students knew they were expected to read, and they could read whatever they wanted—or so it seemed. Dawn had Unfettered Curricular Autonomy, believed in students' academic freedom, and understood that if teachers held power over students, they would not be able to learn. However, in the project just described, she exhibited the type of instructional power one might expect with Dimension III/Protective or even Dimension IV/Disenfranchising.

Now let's look at another classroom teacher: Erin. You met Erin in the Pause to Reflect section earlier in this chapter. I met her during my doctoral studies and became her instructional coach.

Erin had moved from the rural South to a charter high school in the Northeast. Despite our many discussions about power, it was difficult for Erin to conceptualize herself as having power. When asked to define her idea of power, she responded, "I don't feel like there's some power I have and they don't." As I observed her 10th grade English class, I noticed a clear power dynamic that moved easily between teacher and student.

At the beginning of her time at this school, Erin experienced Restricted Curricular Autonomy. The school's goal was to be sure students were prepared for the district end-of-year assessment, and its leadership believed the best way to do this was through heavily scripted lessons expected to move with military-style precision and adherence to outlined timeframes. However, after negotiations with her assistant principal, Erin was able to get more flexibility and experienced Minimal Curricular Autonomy. Her lessons were reviewed by her assistant principal, and her requested revisions might or might not be accepted.

In a lesson about Woodrow Wilson, Erin decided the information students were being asked to learn was incomplete. The portrayal of the former president as a champion of equality failed to address his widely known and documented racist ideologies. As a result, students would have an unbalanced understanding of Wilson, and the history would be misrepresented. Wanting her students to grapple with complex ideas, she revised the lesson to include content that would include Wilson's actual words about African Americans and Asian immigrants. She asked them to consider how they might describe the former president: was he a champion for democracy and freedom or not?

Erin's actions demonstrate how a teacher with restricted and minimal autonomy chose a course of action on behalf of student learning. Although Erin did not believe she had more power than her students, she worked to build their critical thinking and academic agency by making the power-laden decision to go beyond the designated curriculum and provide her students with more accurate historical information. She used her power to give students the opportunity to make a decision about a former president whose beliefs about White people differed greatly from his beliefs about African Americans and Asian immigrants. By presenting more complete information and asking the question "Who was Woodrow Wilson?" she gave students the opportunity to make their own claim and use the evidence presented as support. They had to consider whether the former president could be both a champion of freedom and a racist. Through the broad question Erin asked, they were not being led how to think. The information Erin provided about Wilson's ideologies was meant to guide their understanding and lead them to their own conclusions. She was not protecting her own thinking and guiding her students to join her in that thought.

The examples of Dawn and Erin demonstrate the role power plays in how we convey our beliefs to our students and how we expect them to interact with the curriculum. Here we see how our actions speak louder than our words. Dawn had an environment in terms of curricular autonomy that many would envy and yet chose an academically protective stance with her students. Erin had the more common restricted environment and yet chose an academically agentive stance with her students.

The point is, it is important not to make assumptions about the relationship between levels of autonomy and the dimensions of instructional power. Teachers use power in countless ways in accordance with the ideologies that manifest in the beliefs they hold.

‖ PAUSE TO REFLECT

How Do You Use Power?

Choose a situation in which you had a challenging encounter with a student and answer the following questions:

- What was the race or ethnicity of the student?
- What was the gender of the student?
- Describe the encounter. How did it start? What made it challenging? How far did you go to respond to it (removal of the student from class, referral, etc.)?
- To the extent you are able, identify what underlying beliefs were at play about the student based on factors beyond the child's control (e.g., race/ethnicity, gender, economics).
- How might your underlying beliefs have made the encounter challenging?
- Did your responses to the student reflect your actual beliefs, or did they reflect the beliefs you've been telling yourself you have (e.g., "I don't see color")?
- Were you able to tap into yourself and name your beliefs and how they were shaping this encounter? ▸

Challenging encounters with students often stem from our ideologies about students based on the inherent power differentials related to position and age. Those ideologies get connected to our underlying beliefs about people from various racial and ethnic backgrounds as well as those from various economic backgrounds and those whose gender identities we may disapprove of or not understand. It is crucial for us as teachers to be able to name our ideologies because without doing so, we will never be able to disrupt the behaviors that protect our position and disenfranchise students.

Looking Ahead

In Chapter 3, we will explore the English language to see how it has evolved. Teachers use the English language as both a tool and a weapon, especially with students who are increasing their language repertoire and those who speak what are considered nonstandard dialects. Perspectives about students who use varieties of English become another layer in how instructional power can be used against students.

3 | THE POWER PRINCIPLE AND STUDENT IDENTITIES

But it became increasingly clear how language was both liberating and imprisoning.

— *Toni Morrison*

Language is that *thing* everyone has. It's our calling card, giving people a glimpse into who we may be or where we may be from. When you live in a world where language can shape pop culture and simultaneously be denigrated as wrong or incorrect, then Morrison's words come alive. Many students in many classrooms live Morrison's words every day.

What Are They Talking About?
I Don't Understand

Have you ever found yourself listening to your students and not having a clue what they're talking about? If you're like me, this has happened many times. I found myself asking them to translate—not just the newest slang but words they used during our classroom discussions. It was as if we spoke completely different languages. And by the time I caught on and tried to apply my new learning, I was already behind. They had moved on to something else.

If you know anything about adolescents, you know they like to experiment with words. Working with adolescents is a guarantee that we as adults will, at some point, be completely clueless regarding what our students are saying. We will find ourselves linguistically cut off and searching for ways into their conversations. Finding ways into my students' conversations meant finding ways into their culture. As we saw in Chapter 2, culture is central to identity, and in this chapter, we will explore the inseparability of language, culture, and identity.

The value we place on the English language and how we believe students should use their words in school influence what we think about them as people, their capacity to be successful in school, and how we allow them to use language as a form of expression. A teacher I spoke with offered this response when asked to describe how she believed students should speak in school: "But you know it's the fact that like people are observing them, people are listening to them, and this is school, and so you should show you're educated." The statement suggests that there is a right way to speak at school, and the use of speech that does not fit the paradigm is wrong and shows a lack of education. To be honest, many of us have subscribed to this idea and, as we will see, the effects on students can be devastating.

Before we talk about English specifically, we need to discuss language more broadly. As social theorist Raymond Williams (1977) explains, "A definition of language is always, implicitly or explicitly, a definition of human beings in the world" (p. 21). Language is one of the defining elements of a culture and serves to give people a place within a particular group. It marks where people come from and is foundational to one's identity. Language is a placeholder and veritable "seat marker" in society, which can often determine how far a person is allowed to go in life. Education researcher Michael Stubbs (2002) states, "We hear language through a powerful filter of social values and stereotypes" (p. 66). Once we hear someone speak, we immediately go through a mental checklist of items about who the person is and where that person may be from; we speculate about educational background, and, if we're really honest with ourselves, we think about occupation and income bracket. This is what we do with adults.

Stop right here and think about the last adult stranger you talked to. What went through your head the moment you heard that person speak? Did the person have an unfamiliar accent—an accent you tried to place? Did something in the way they used their words cause you even the slightest bit of concern? What about education? Was this something you thought about as you listened? If you're like me, you had questions. You began to make assumptions about that person. Their use of language told you something about them and affected your thinking about them.

If this is our typical knee-jerk reaction to adults, imagine how our internal mechanisms can affect how we approach our teaching of students whose language and use of words sit outside what we believe to be correct or right. Our thinking about language and how it should be used at school holds power over how we direct our students' speech. The question is, why do we hold so tightly to this thing called English? Why do we hold students hostage to something many of us don't even realize is its own variant of a language?

We've discussed ideology earlier, in other contexts, and it applies here as well. As we demand students adhere to fixed ideas about the way they should speak, we're using a belief system many of us do not question. This behavior represents a lack of questioning, or what is known as adopting "common sense" assumptions (Gramsci, 1971) about ideas accepted as truth without questioning their origins or the reasons behind the acceptance. Therefore, the idea that there is a right way and a wrong way to speak English, especially in school, is accepted as truth, with rarely a consideration as to why.

Before we move forward, let's take a brief step back and discuss American English and how it has come to shape our national identity. So much of what we think and do is based on habits of mind we have not taken the time to interrogate. In discussing American English, we get to ask some important questions about how we understand and use our instructional power in ways that often alienate children and cut them off from the learning process.

This Thing Called "English"

This thing we call English must be understood in the context of its origins. As the American colonies separated from England and became the United States, one of the founders, John Adams, believed it was necessary to have a form of language that would create an identity unique to the new nation. Yes, the English roots would still be present; however, there would be something different about the way in which this new nation would use language (Heath, 1992; Kahne, 1992). Adams petitioned his political allies to institute an American form of English and have it structured around forms of grammar that would be written down to create a standard of American speech—hence one element of our concept of standard American English. As Adams was shaping his ideals about American English around the use of structured grammar, another set of principles was at work to shape standards of American English. This belief was grounded in the idea that standard American English should be shaped by the ways early Americans used speech in their daily lives.

At the outset of this American dialect of English, it was meant to be the language of the common person. Our brand of English was forged to break away from the formality of British English, which made social mobility very difficult. A person's accent was a clear determinant of social class and perceived intellect. Language—or one's accent—was synonymous with a person's position and dictated how far a person could advance in society. The goal of American English was accessibility, eliminating language as an easy marker of one's station in life, as it was in England. American English was to be used to forge an identity, not reveal one's position. The language was to be available to all members of society equally, to create unity. Gravin (as quoted in Dilliard, 1975) explains, "good" English meant English "without recognizable stereotypes or geographic features" (p. 59). In its early stage of development, American English was a linguistic outcast—or, in the words of Kahne (1992), "a colonial substandard" (p. 212). Identity as an American was the goal, not being able to determine where a person was from—geographically or socially.

Although much credit is given to Daniel Webster for publishing the first American dictionary in 1828, he actually followed in the footsteps of Samuel Johnson, who had developed a dictionary about 50 years earlier, as the nation was beginning to take shape as fully independent from British rule. Just as Adams had been working toward shaping the language as an identity unifier, Johnson, one of Adams's peers, worked to solidify the American way of speaking by putting it on paper. He thereby created the structure around which Americans could begin to understand themselves as a people whose use of words was independent from that of their oppressors. Johnson's dictionary was significant in that it became one of the identity markers of what it meant to be an American through the spoken and written word.

What must be understood at this point is that given the structure of American society at its outset, the American form of speech and writing was not meant for the enslaved or Indigenous people, who were not considered members of society. Therefore, any discussion about the form of American speech also carries the weight of exclusion. However, what must also be understood is the inevitability of cultural and linguistic exchange among people. As Africans were forced into enslavement and stripped of their home languages, they had to adopt unfamiliar structures of speech and communication. Being able to speak in English became necessary for survival. The same was true for Indigenous Americans. They had to learn English in order to survive as the country they inhabited became something altogether different.

As enslaved Africans were forced to use American English, they developed a unique brand of the language that has evolved over time and become what is known as African American Vernacular English (AAVE). The point here is not one of linguistic history; rather, it is important to have a sense of how language evolves and operates. It is equally important to understand that what we call English is a variant of a preexisting language and, through cultural exchanges (forced or otherwise), has many variants of its own.

Language, Culture, and Race

There is no mistaking the relationship between language, culture, and race, particularly in the United States. Given our history, ideologies about race are evident in all aspects of society, including school. Language, being a marker of identity, is no different. In a slightly revised version of the earlier quote from Stubbs (2002), I believe we hear language through the lens of culture and stereotype. How people use their language allows us to place them in a group most associated with their form of speech.

Formerly enslaved Africans developed AAVE on the basis of their original African languages and through cultural interaction with their enslavers and even interaction with Indigenous Americans. Despite being characterized as its own variant of English, AAVE is often viewed as a broken form of English, as many of its structures defy those deemed as standard in American English. Much of the consternation around the characterization of AAVE rests on the shoulders of what Ibram X. Kendi calls "racist ideologies that lead to racist principles" (2016, p. 22). Thomas Jefferson, considered the crafter of America's notions of freedom and liberty, believed "the blacks are inferior to the whites in the endowments both of body and mind" (1787, p. 143). As a founder of many principles and original laws of the United States, Jefferson was instrumental in weaving and instituting ideologies that continue to shape much of the thinking about Black people today. Because the nation's foundation rests on the belief that people of African descent are inherently inferior, their use of language is also seen through the lens of inferiority.

As the saying goes, necessity is the mother of invention. Although equal access to language shaped the origins of American English, the ability to write is what standardized this variant. Unfortunately, laws made learning to read and write illegal for the enslaved, but the need to communicate necessitated language development through cultural exchange. Mixing the standardized form of American English with the varieties of African languages created a version of English that, although structured, was considered substandard.

Part of being seen as African American has become inextricably linked to language use. As a self-identified African American woman, I use many variants of AAVE as well as traditionally characterized forms of standard English, and I recognize that my identity as a Black woman is tied to how I use language. My language is my identity. It is my culture, and there is no separation between them. Unfortunately, I am keenly aware of the linguistic undervaluing that people who identify as African American face when they use AAVE.

Language and the Power Principle in the Classroom

"Teacher talk and student talk are essential components that determine the quality of learning in the classroom. When there is distance between them, other kinds of strife develop" (Kohl, 2002, p. 147). Kohl's words shape this section as we explore how teachers' language ideologies influence their use of instructional power in the classroom.

One of the most difficult realizations educators must make is that they view their students' language through different lenses, using varying scales of value. Yet, as we know, teachers will tell you they view every child the same—and on the surface, they will mean what they say. Unfortunately, as I've stated in previous chapters, decades of research demonstrate otherwise. This finding is particularly true with White teachers of African American students (Downey & Pribesh, 2004).

The challenge is that for centuries we have determined that American English is a fixed form of speech, and anything with sounds outside the structure is wrong and must be repaired. Not only does the "broken" speech have to be repaired; also the speaker is somehow deficient and lacking in intellect. This notion that speech determines station in life has been carried forward to our schools, and as Stubbs points out, our values shape how we think about and often interact with those whose form of English varies not only from our own, but from what we consider to be good, correct, standard English. If we're honest with ourselves, when we hear a variation of English we consider incorrect, particularly in a place we deem formal, we have a natural reaction that tells a lot about our ideologies about language.

Shelving Language Identity

Let's revisit Amy from Chapter 1. Her story is salient here because it demonstrates the significance of language ideologies on the use of instructional power. Amy believed there were definite right and wrong ways to speak, especially at school. Because of this ideology, she corrected her students whenever she heard them speak a non-school-sanctioned dialect of English. Amy is the teacher I referred to earlier in this chapter, who explained her rationale about why she corrected her students' speech in the following words: "But you know it's the fact that like people are observing them, people are listening to them, and this is a school, and so you should show you're educated." In her mind, being educated had an associated sound, and when that sound violated her common sense beliefs—her ideologies and understanding of what educated people should sound like, especially in school—her response was to fix what she saw as a problem. Amy had a clear ideology about how kids should use words in class because language and the use of words demonstrates what it means to sound educated. School was the place where students *should* sound educated. As a teacher, Amy held to the belief that it was her job to make sure students spoke in educated ways.

The curriculum in Amy's school was highly restricted. Her lesson plans were developed by an instructional coach, and she was expected to follow the lessons to the letter, with little to no flexibility. In Chapter 1, we discussed the Power Principle matrix and how context is a factor in where teachers might begin enacting their instructional power. In Chapter 2, we discussed how the relationship between teachers' beliefs and actions intersect with their educational context and determine where they might land in the matrix shown in Figure 1.1. In Amy's case, we would expect her to automatically land in either Dimension III/Protective or Dimension IV/Disenfranchising. It was her decision to exercise her power in alienating ways that sealed her location in Dimension IV. Her instructional environment was highly constrained, and her use of power was negative, creating a setting where students' use of language was highly controlled based on her beliefs—or ideology—about the English language.

As I learned more about Amy's language ideology and related need to control, it was clear her beliefs stemmed from her own schooling. She grew up in a small town in the Northeast that was largely White and middle class, with very little racial or ethnic diversity. Amy fit the predominant demographic of U.S. teachers: White, middle class, and holding a particular sensibility about school that many students of color do not share. In our discussion about her expectations for how students should speak in her classroom, she said, "Well, as far as them . . . I don't want them using incorrect grammar. When I hear it, I correct them every time." When I later visited her class, I saw that she had described her ideologies about English with great precision. She corrected her students *every* time she heard them use a form of English she deemed incorrect and had them restate their sentence.

Remember the book-return scenario in Chapter 1? Let's look at it through the lens of Amy's language ideology and her use of instructional power. Jake borrowed a book and completed Part A of the checkout process but did not execute the full process because he forgot to write down the return date before returning the book to the shelf. Let's consider the first part of the exchange between Amy and Jake to show how Amy's language ideology intersected with her instructional power and shaped the interaction:

> Amy: Jake, where's the book?
>
> Jake: It's on the shelf.
>
> Amy: I don't see the return date on the form, so the book's not back.
>
> Jake: Look at the first book on the shelf. I been turn't that in. I forgot to write the date down.
>
> Amy: You were supposed to write the date on the list to check it back in before putting it back on the shelf . . . And it's "I turned it in already," not "I been turn't. . . . Please say it correctly.
>
> Jake: I turned it in already.

Why was there a need to change what the student said? In telling Jake he needed to say his statement correctly, Amy signaled a few things. First, there is a definite right and wrong way to use language; second, his way was the wrong way; and third, only rigidly defined "correct" forms of English would be allowed in her classroom.

II PAUSE TO REFLECT

How Does Language Ideology Affect Your Instructional Power?

Given this discussion about language ideologies, it's important to think about how your beliefs about language intersect with the way you use your instructional power. Ask yourself the following questions:

- What do I believe about how students should be allowed to speak in school?
- When I reflect on my own use of words in school, do I use only school-sanctioned varieties of English?
- How do my beliefs about language influence my expectations of my students?
- Where might I have used my instructional power in alienating ways against my students? ▶

In Amy's case, she had no control over the lessons she had to teach; her curricular autonomy was restricted. Her beliefs about what being educated sounds like and her role in making that happen in her classroom dictated the decisions she made regarding how her students were allowed to speak; she disregarded their use of English varieties. Amy was also influenced by her personal beliefs and background, which included only the dominant cultural variety of English—that is, a form of speaking that would be considered formal and school-sanctioned. As a member of the dominant culture, she tried to force her students into this dominant way of speaking as a way to help them be and sound "educated." Consider these additional comments from Amy:

> But I tell them all the time, are you gonna say that on a job interview? Like how unprofessional do you look? Honestly, it seems like

> it's not worth it, because then the moment that they leave, they either
> go right back talking their way or speaking the way that they were or
> they're hearing even other teachers speak like *that.*

Amy heard her students' and colleagues' language through her filter of social value and stereotype. Although her words appear harsh
here, on this page (and they are), it is important to be honest with
yourself and admit you may harbor some of the same sentiments.
You may even have used your instructional power in ways to signal
to your students that their way of speaking has no place in school.

Amy's curricular autonomy was clearly restricted, *and* she
enacted a disenfranchising approach to her instruction. Her students
had no leeway in their speech—a situation that amounted to shelving
their identity. Thus Amy's classes resided in a Dimension IV/Disen-
franchising environment.

Let's agree on a critical truth: students are keenly aware of the
messages we teachers send. Even when we're not aware of the impact
of our words, our students pick up their meaning. When, like Amy, we
use what Devereaux (2015) calls a *correctionist* framework to express
disdain for how our students speak, we communicate loud and clear
something about our students' identity, their culture, and their race
or ethnicity. Consider a Latina/o/x high school student whom I will
call Isabela, who had this to say about her perception of her teachers:

> They force you to write a certain way, and I'm not saying it's by the
> way they're teaching us, but I just think that if some of us speak
> a little slang, it's an issue. They say things like, "you can't talk like
> that," "you can't write that because that's not proper English."

The teachers in Isabela's school, which was in the Northeast,
were predominantly White. As I questioned her a bit more, she
revealed that she and her friends were constantly forced to change
their speech both in and outside the classroom. The attempts to control use of language was pervasive. Many teachers in the building sent
a clear message that Isabela's and her friends' use of language—and
thus their identity—was wrong and not accepted in school.

It is fair to assume that the teachers believed they had good intentions and were trying to help their students become better speakers. However, as a person I highly respect once told me, "The road to hell is paved with good intentions." When students are constantly told they must speak "proper" English, they learn that their language and thus their identity are not welcomed in school. They learn how to shelve their identities, which makes connecting to school difficult and comes with implications for achievement. Shelving linguistic identity is something many students of color face—both native speakers of English and students adopting English as part of their speech repertoire.

Supporting Language Identity

What does it look like when a teacher has a perspective on the use of English varieties in the classroom that differs from the perspectives we've just examined? When students are not required to shelve their linguistic identity? What ideology is at play when a teacher realizes there is no absolute right or wrong way to use English, especially in non-content-specific linguistic interactions? For an example, let's return to Erin, who was introduced in Chapter 2, and her AP language class.

Erin held a wide perspective on how students should use language in her class; she did not subscribe to a correctionist framework. In watching her teach, it became clear students were allowed latitude in how they could speak and use their words. Now, because this was an AP language class and students were preparing for their AP exams, I expected they would be required to speak in school-sanctioned varieties of English. Nothing could have been further from the truth. Students engaged in a smorgasbord of language varieties as they discussed themes from Shakespeare's *Oedipus Rex*. As students used versions of African American English coupled with their local colloquialisms and "standard" English, Erin stood back and made her presence known only to push student thinking and make sure they were addressing the questions posed in the class. None of the cross sections of language varieties impeded students' ability to make sense of their reading or the assignment, which was written in "standard" English. Here's a glimpse into Erin's class (using pseudonyms for students' names):

> Erin: What's happening between Oedipus, Jocasta, and Creon at this point in the play?
>
> Marcus: Well, I'ma say it like this. . . . The whole thing was 'effed up, cuz, like, who wanna have to choose between they family members? I mean, Creon is, like, constantly tryna do some undercover, hide-in-the-back stuff. Like with Tiresias. . . .
>
> Maria: Right. . . . Especially since, like, Oedipus is the king, but, like, Creon . . . Nah. He shaddy. I 'on't trust him. Like I know he's acting like everything is cool, but I still think he might be up to something.
>
> Erin: What other ideas are there to add to this?
>
> Mike: Well, here's my take on it. First of all . . . I think Jocasta is trying to get everybody to chill. I mean, Oedipus is trying to banish her brother. Oedipus is hotheaded and reacts quickly to stuff. I mean yes, Creon is trying to prove himself as loyal and Oedipus was about to, like, have him banished and Jocasta is wanting to be, like, calm and stuff.

From this exchange, 1 learned a few things. First, I wished I had understood Sophocles this clearly when I was that age! More important, however, it was clear the students were fully immersed in the characters and the relationships between them, and the mix of language varieties did not interfere with their understanding. And lastly, Erin's willingness to let them speak in the way they felt most comfortable in no way hindered her ability to get a sense of their meaning making, which was the goal.

When I asked Erin why she did not correct her students' speech, she explained her ideology as follows:

> I think I have what I think is a true understanding of language and how language is used. I have the understanding that people use language to communicate, to relate; it's very familial. I guess this is where I'm exercising my power, because I get pretty irate when I

> hear people tell students, "That's not the correct quote-unquote way to talk. That's not right." That's part of people's identities, and how can you tell them that the way that they identify is wrong? . . . And then I'm also bringing in my background knowledge of how language was stripped from African Americans. . . . You know, they took their whole language, but then they still found a way to develop their own sense of language even with theirs being taken away; but then you wanna get mad at how these kids use language from home. So for me to tell people like the way that you relate when I definitely know when I go home, this is the how we communicate in family, like to tell somebody you're wrong for me is disrespectful.

Erin's ideology about school-based use of language is rooted in her own identity as a woman of African descent with a keen sense of the historical context around which African Americans acquired language in what became the United States. Just as founder John Adams realized that language was a critical factor in shaping one's identity, Erin applied the same ideology to her understanding about the importance of language in the way she allowed students to use language in her class. As students engaged with their content, they learned that language is driven largely by audience and purpose. Although Erin led an AP English class, her approach to how students use speech is applicable to all content areas.

Like Amy, whose teaching environment was in the Restricted Curricular Autonomy category, Erin worked in a school district where teachers were expected to follow a prescribed curriculum, especially in 10th grade, a grade in which high-stakes tests were administered. Unlike Amy, Erin had Calibrated Curricular Autonomy, which allowed her to make choices about what students would read and what assignments they would complete, as long as she could demonstrate adherence to the state's learning standards.

Erin's CCA environment and use of instructional power placed her in the Dimension II/Agentive quadrant of the Power Principle matrix. Her district had curricular expectations; however, her language ideology and use of instructional power helped students build educational agency as she afforded them space to be their full linguistic selves. She did not force them to shelve their identities. Instead, their identities were on full display as tools to create meaning about their content. Students were also able to use their language as bridges to skill development.

Through Erin's example, we learn that as students engage with content, how they use their spoken speech versus their written speech should be governed by the communication structures of the content, audience, and purpose. Erin teaches us the importance of not forcing students into false structures of language use by requiring "standard" English to engage with content.

From Amy and Erin, we learn how teachers' use of their instructional power can build students' educational agency or create disenfranchising environments. Although many people may consider this discussion about the use of English as something specific to the English/language arts classroom, students across all disciplines face the possible shelving of their linguistic identities. Despite the origins of the American form of English, the belief in a standard form is rooted in the hearts and minds of many people—especially teachers. This belief leads to actions that are alienating and ultimately disenfranchising to many students, but especially to students of color.

Identifying Your Quadrant

In Chapter 1, you spent time defining your power principle ideology. In Chapter 2, you worked on looking at your educational and cultural histories. Now let's focus on language-use policies in your school, your personal language-use policy as evidenced in your classroom and your lesson design, and how you may be using your instructional power. If you realize your context and use of instructional power lands you in Dimension III/Protective or Dimension IV/Disenfranchising in the Power Principle matrix, questions in the Pause to Reflect section will help you move toward more effective uses of your instructional power, landing you in the quadrant for Dimension II/ Agentive or Dimension I/Empowering.

To begin the work of identifying your quadrant, conduct a personal Power Principle study. Choose a different class each day for the next two or three days. For each class, do the following:

1. Track the number of times you corrected your students' spoken speech.
2. Track the number of times you corrected your students' written speech.
3. Track which students you corrected.
4. Track which students you did not correct.
5. Notice and record any student responses to your correction.

Now respond to the questions in the Pause to Reflect section.

II PAUSE TO REFLECT

**How Do You Use Instructional Power
in Terms of Language Use?**

- Review your data. What stood out to you?
  - Did you correct your students' spoken language?
    - Why did you correct spoken language?
    - When did you most often correct spoken language?
    - How did you correct spoken language?
    - How did your students respond to being corrected?
  - Did you correct your students' written language?
    - Why did you correct written language?
    - When did you most often correct written language?
    - How did you correct written language?
    - How did your students respond to being corrected?
  - Based on your responses to these questions, in which quadrant/power dimension did you most often operate?

- What does the quadrant/power dimension in which you most often operated reveal about your language ideology?
- Based on what you noticed from your students' reactions to being corrected, how is your language ideology affecting them? How is it affecting your relationships with them?
- Based on the quadrant/power dimension in which you most often operated during this exercise, how is your language ideology affecting your instruction?
- Did you have an explicit policy on language use in your classroom?
  - If so, how did you communicate this to your students?
  - If not, how did you communicate your hidden policy? ▸

Affirmative Language Support

Now that we've covered ground on what harmful language correction looks like, let's pivot and examine affirmative linguistic support. The decision to correct or not correct a student's use of language should be based on purpose and an understanding of why students are using a particular language variety over another. For adolescents, language variety comes with the territory as students try on language as a form of identity development and a way to separate themselves as independent beings from the adults in their lives—mostly their parents.

If students are in a general conversation with peers, there is *never* a need to adopt a correctionist framework. Let students speak. Students should be free, or as one teacher I worked with would say, "let your freak vibe fly." There are even times when students are using a language variety while demonstrating knowledge, and correcting student speech is more harmful than useful.

Let's revisit Erin's lesson. Her students used a combination of formal school-based English and their home language to demonstrate understanding of the text. As Erin supported her students, she used an English variety to reinforce student knowledge as well. If this lesson included formal essay writing, students would need to adjust their speech to adhere to the structures of that task. In this instance, students would benefit from Erin's support in helping them build a bridge between their most familiar language variety and the language variety required for formal writing. Recall her students' use of language during the lesson on *Oedipus Rex:*

> Marcus: Well, I'ma say it like this. . . . The whole thing was 'effed up, cuz, like, who wanna have to choose between they family members? I mean, Creon is, like, constantly tryna do some undercover, hide-in-the-back stuff. Like with Tiresias. . . .

> Maria: Right. . . . Especially since, like, Oedipus is the king, but, like, Creon . . . Nah. He shaddy. I 'on't trust him. Like I know he's acting like everything is cool, but I still think he might be up to something.

To prepare her students for formal/structured writing, Erin could do several things to foster honoring of their understanding and their language:

- Acknowledge their understanding by asking them for evidence from the text to support their view (e.g., "What makes you think Creon is up to something? Why don't you trust him?"). (Responding to students' answers to these questions, Erin would speak back to her students using the formal register needed for their writing without correcting them or making them feel as though how they spoke was somehow wrong.)
- Ask what students meant by the colloquialisms they used to further anchor their understanding and how they related to the discussion.
- Introduce the next phase of their work, the formal essay, and discuss how language in a formal essay would differ from the language used in their classroom discussion.
- Model for students how to move from the colloquial to the formal in writing, and begin a discussion about the difference. Here's an example of such modeling:

Colloquialism: "I'ma say it like this. . . . The whole thing was 'effed up."

Formal structure: "As I read this portion of *Oedipus*, the situation appears problematic."

Prompts to understand the difference: What do you notice about the use of words? What do you notice about the sentences?

Conducting an inquiry into the language builds students' knowledge of formal structures, increases analytical skills, and allows them to see their language as having its own structure alongside formal structures. The inquiry is an academic way of honoring varieties of the English language.

If students demonstrate knowledge using their English variety in a way that makes it difficult for a teacher to know whether they understand disciplinary concepts, then it is indeed necessary to push them toward the correct disciplinary language as a means of demonstrating content knowledge and mastery. This approach is particularly important in science and math domains as misused words can be the difference between accuracy and inaccuracy.

Looking Ahead

In this chapter, we focused on language ideologies and how they relate to instructional practices. Reflections prompted you to capture your own language ideology and consider how it affects your instructional practices and your use of instructional power, and how those may be influencing your student relationships. As we move through the coming chapters, continue to be mindful of your ideology and how you use your instructional power to direct students.

4 | THE POWER PRINCIPLE: BEYOND ENGLISH LANGUAGE ARTS

I am not a reading teacher.

I cannot tell you how many times I've heard this statement from teachers of math, social studies, and science. It's as though reading only matters if you teach English language arts; as if students do not read in any other class.

Let me set the record straight. If you're reading this book and you teach a subject other than English language arts, you are correct: you are not a reading teacher. In fact, English language arts teachers do not want you to teach students how to read, per se. What they want is your support for literacy by helping your students learn how to read *in your subject*. I say this as someone who has been on the receiving end of comments as a teacher, a coach, and a consultant.

I fully understand why teachers in other subject areas feel the need to make it plain that they are not reading teachers; but not being a person whose job it is to teach children how to read does not negate the reality that the reading process permeates your classroom. Just for the sake of clarity, English is a subject and language arts is the skill students apply *across many subject areas* to build literacy.

Back to Stubbs: "We hear language through a powerful filter of social values and stereotypes" (2002, p. 66). This filter exists in all areas of school. Until we teachers, regardless of content area, admit that we have an internal framework related to how students should speak, our students will continue to be subject to the hidden curriculum against which we judge them. By "hidden curriculum," I mean the expectations we hold for students without telling them. The hidden curriculum consists of those silent criteria we use to evaluate students based on our ideologies; however, our students do not know they are being judged and held accountable to what is in our heads because the criteria are not formally communicated (Alsubaie, 2015; Giroux & Penna, 1979).

Power differentials exist in all areas of life, especially where there are inherent differences based on factors such as age, experience, perceived knowledge, and position. Positionally, the teacher-student relationship is primed for protective and disenfranchising enactments of power. This is particularly true in classes where students are learning new content and acquiring unfamiliar skills. At least in the English language arts classroom, students come equipped with the baseline skill—that of the general language base upon which other content and subject-based skills are built. But other disciplines have their own vocabularies, which convey the conceptual understandings students need to develop to demonstrate mastery of the material. Students must learn the disciplinary language, which may be completely new. They must also build understanding about the operational aspects in order to do the work of the discipline. They must be able to answer, as McConachie and Petrosky (2009) suggest in their work on disciplinary literacy, "what does it mean to think like [a scientist]. . . how do [historians] function to achieve the goals of the discipline?" Although these questions live in the English language arts world, they seem to take more of a front seat in the other disciplines. The question is, how does the Power Principle operate in disciplines other than English language arts if the focus may not be on how students are speaking or writing?

Looking Beyond ELA

Whatever the discipline, the question remains: how does power drive the adult inputs and student outputs? It all comes down to the ideologies that shape our beliefs. What you believe about your content and the students you teach shapes how you deliver the content and the learning experiences.

Consider this example. Several years back, a mother contacted me with concerns about her son's math class. Her son explained the class in the following way:

1. The teacher comes into the classroom and asks the students to take out their homework.

2. The teacher goes through the homework, giving the answers to each of the problems, and asks students to raise their hand to show who got the answer right and who got it wrong.

3. Then the teacher shows the next thing, tells students what it is, and does a few problems on the board.

4. After that, the teacher directs students' attention to the practice problems in the book and tells them which problems to complete.

5. The teacher goes to her desk while students complete their work. Students are allowed to go to the teacher and ask questions.

6. Before class ends, the teacher assigns the homework for students to finish.

The mother believed her son was capable but needed the teacher to offer more active instruction to support his learning. She was also concerned because her son had said he felt purposely ignored by the teacher for reasons related to his race. He was one of 2 African American boys in a class of 15 students, and the teacher was White. I advised the mother to schedule a meeting with the teacher and ask her to share her philosophy.

Here's what the mother shared with me. The teacher was reluctant to meet with her, but after several requests, a conference was finally scheduled. The teacher said she believed that students in an advanced class, such as the one the boy was in, should be able to pick up the concepts quickly. She informed the parent that students have every opportunity to ask questions during their practice time, and if a child does not ask during that time, she assumes the concept was understood. The mother tried to explain that her son enjoyed the class because he liked math, and until that point, he had performed quite well in math classes as well as on the standardized tests (scoring above 90 percent, the recommended threshold for entry into the class). This parent had reason to feel confident in her child's ability to do the work, especially if a teacher took the time to show how to do the work in different ways. The mother explained that her son liked to explore various ways to problem solve and was interested in the connections between concepts. In response, the teacher said she had been teaching algebra for several years and was confident in her ability to get kids to perform successfully. She went on to suggest that if the mother was concerned about the way the teacher approached teaching, perhaps transferring her son to a more appropriately leveled class would be best. There was no acknowledgment of the child's need to understand concepts. The teacher held to a performance mentality that expected students to complete problems related to a particular concept at hand, take the test, and move to the next concept.

Although this example may seem shocking, the situation is common, especially in math, with research showing teachers use the idea of providing no support in advanced classes as a tool to weed students out instead of actively engaging them in the learning process (Delpit, 2012; Martin, 2012; McGee & Martin, 2011). Research has also shown the subtleties of teachers' actions and messages sent through their words, particularly for students of color, where the pervading sentiment is they do not belong in advanced classes (Howard & Reynolds, 2008; Steele, 2010). All students perform at the level of their teacher's expectations, and this is particularly true for students of color—and even more so for African American male students.

Let's unpack the described scenario through the lens of the Power Principle. The teacher gave no indication about the degree to which she was adhering to a prescribed curriculum or whether she had restrictions on what she could teach. From this perspective, the curricular dimension was not necessarily at play. The school was a private school, which may have been the reason why the teacher did not use the curriculum as the pedagogical excuse. Instead, she went directly to her beliefs, which I think was brave and helped the parent fully understand what she might need to do for her son's academic success and possible emotional safety. The teacher's belief statement made it clear that she held to one of the core characteristics of Dimension IV/Disenfranchising instructional power. She believed there was only one way for the class to operate. She also seemed to be expressing an ideology that some students are smart and others are not quite smart enough.

Teachers' need to explain their years of experience and confidence in their methods characterizes Dimension III/Protective instructional power. When parents/caregivers question teachers about their practice, teachers often find it necessary to let parents know how many years they have been teaching as a defense mechanism against what feels like a professional threat. The sense of professional threat triggers a response meant to send the message that "I know what I'm doing. I've been at this for a very long time." Often this stance is used with parents/caregivers whom a teacher feels need to be put in their place. The teacher has to let the parents/caregivers know who's in charge of the classroom—and ultimately, who is in charge of their children. Such stances are taken with families from all walks of life, but most often with families of color, and according to research, most often with Black families and families experiencing economic instability (Bridges et al., 2012).

The thinking in these situations goes back to embedded ideologies about who belongs in school and who does not. Such thinking also relates to the idea of who has the right to question professionals and who does not. These perceptions cross racial lines among teachers but are seen most often with White teachers as they engage with people of color. The belief here is that the teachers are the professionals, which we can all agree they are; however, this thinking is rooted in professional privilege layered by other social factors, including race and economics.

Moment of truth: I must admit my own guilt of such thinking and had to do a lot of unpacking about my own beliefs and how they were disenfranchising families as they sought to better understand their child's progress in my class. As you reflect on your own practice, think about how you are communicating your beliefs about your pedagogy and your years in the profession, and if you are unwittingly disenfranchising the most important educational partner your students need: the parent or caregiver.

In another aspect of the described scenario, the teacher's need to move so quickly to telling the parent it might be best for her child and the other children to remove the student and place him in a "more appropriately leveled class" spoke volumes about how she approached her profession and the students in the class. The teacher believed some students belonged in an advanced math class and others did not, and it was her responsibility to weed out those who did not belong. Here again the teacher exhibited Dimension III/Protective instructional power, acting to protect the "sanctity" of the level of the class. The teacher did not give any information about the child and focused the discussion on herself and her instructional approach. She made no attempt to try to understand what the student needed or how she might make adjustments to foster a more welcoming learning environment. The most support students had was that they were allowed to go to the teacher's desk with questions.

Students should be able to speak up for themselves and ask questions, but if the message is "I'm going to my desk and if you have a question about your work, you come to me," the likelihood of a student going to the teacher greatly diminishes. Who wants to look like they do not know what they're doing in front of their peers? Adults are not inclined to do so; therefore, it stands to reason a middle schooler would also not want to do so.

Let's look at this situation from the student side: Your teacher reviews the homework and asks you to raise your hand if you got the problem under review right and to raise your hand if you got the problem wrong. If you got it right, the response is "OK. Good." If you got it wrong, you're not asked why; you simply raise your hand to inform the world of your momentary mathematical ineptitude. Your teacher simply moves on and you're left not gaining any understanding. The so-called lesson consists of the teacher telling you what you're learning, putting problems on the board, and then assigning practice problems that you and your classmates are left to complete on your own. You move forward and then—snag—you come to a problem you are not quite sure you fully understand. Do you get out of your seat and expose yourself to your classmates to walk up to the teacher's desk? Chances are, you do not. You sit in your chair and hope for the best. Wash. Rinse. Repeat.

From an instructional power perspective, this is a disenfranchising learning environment. The process is rigid, and students can't move or operate outside the teacher's structure. They are expected to become vulnerable enough to share their misunderstandings; however, there is no evidence the teacher will follow through by providing support. The teacher leads from the front, literally. Those students who demonstrate the success components valued by this teacher are most likely to get most of her attention, and those who may be experiencing difficulty are left to themselves. The student in the scenario relied on his peers for support. Students were left to fend for themselves. They formed academic alliances, and each member of the alliance had to hope the other members had the knowledge they needed at any given time in the learning sequence.

Some may argue this process is best for separating the chaff from the wheat, which is a common pedagogical approach in math; however, far too many students are having their opportunity to learn diminished. Far too many are developing negative math identities and losing out on something they might actually be quite skilled at (Gholson & Wilkes, 2017; Martin, 2012).

As educators build learning environments, they must consider the seen and unseen components of the curriculum. The hidden curriculum (Alsubaie, 2015; Giroux & Penna, 1979) carries as much weight as the known or enacted curriculum because it reflects the ideologies of the teacher against which students are measured. When poorly informed and based on bias, the hidden curriculum can create a disenfranchising environment for learners because it leads them to develop low esteem with regard to learning and often reinforces what Steele (2010) calls a *stereotype threat.*

With stereotype threat, students display the actions associated with common racialized and ethnic tropes about them. This behavior is akin to rising to expectations but goes a bit further. In his study, Steele found instances when a White boy was told he was playing basketball to assess his ability and would underperform. Conversely, if the same child was told he was playing basketball for fun, his skills were better than when he was assessed on the skill. The same was true for African American students who were being assessed in math.

If they were told they were to complete a set of problems for the sole purpose of developing problem-solving skills versus being assessed to determine their math aptitude, the students who were asked to problem solve fared as well as their White and Asian counterparts. In both cases, the common stereotype about who is considered good at something prevailed.

In the described scenario, being one of only 2 Black students in a class of 15, with the rest being White, is environmentally threatening enough. The feeling that you don't belong because there are so few people who look like you creates social dis-ease. Couple this feeling with a teacher who seemingly adopts a Darwinian approach to learning, and it is easy to see how disenfranchising the environment can be for students.

ǁ PAUSE TO REFLECT

How Might You Be Enacting a Protective or Disenfranchising Environment in Your Classroom?

You've had the opportunity to consider several critical elements in a Dimension III/Protective and a Dimension IV/Disenfranchising environment. To help you understand how you might be creating such an environment in your classroom, respond to the following questions:

- When asked to meet with families/caregivers, are you reluctant? If so, what might your reluctance signal?
- When meeting with families/caregivers, how likely are you to mention your years of experience? How likely are you to think about your years of experience?
- What differences do you notice in your interactions with families/caregivers if they have less education than you?

- What differences do you notice in your interactions with families/caregivers from different socioeconomic backgrounds than yours?
- What differences do you notice in your interactions with families/caregivers when they differ racially or ethnically from you?
- If you teach an advanced class, how often have you suggested a student be moved to a "lower-level" course? Which students have you been most likely to suggest this for?
- How rigid are you regarding the policies and procedures in your classroom?
- What rules might you be holding students to that have not been expressly communicated to them (hidden curriculum)? ▶

Your responses to the reflection questions reveal where you are in your thinking and how you might be subtly protecting yourself in the face of what might be perceived professional threat. When parents/caregivers request conferences to discuss their child's progress, we often feel as though we are under attack. The U.S. system of education has long operated from the perspective that teachers know best what a child needs in terms of learning, even if they feel constrained by hierarchical pressures such as state initiatives, excessive testing, and rigid curricula. Additionally, many teachers hold deficit ideologies about groups of people from different racial, ethnic, and socioethnic backgrounds. Studies have shown that White parents from all economic and educational backgrounds are more likely to be granted access to schools (e.g., conferences, PTA membership) than parents of children from other groups regardless of their economic and educational backgrounds (Bridges et al., 2012; Howard, 2015;

Howard & Reynolds, 2008). Unfortunately, African American parents continue to face the greatest obstacles when attempting to learn about their child's progress—a reality that is both anecdotally and empirically confirmed. A historically embedded societal fear of African Americans pervades schools across the United States; therefore, when Black parents attempt to learn about their children in school, they are often met with the effects of this underlying fear, with teachers projecting a Protective dimension of instructional power. The underlying belief continues to be that only certain parents deserve to question teachers' practices and others do not.

If your first response when a child in an advanced class struggles is to suggest the child should be moved, you may need to stop and consider the roots of such thinking. Thank goodness theories about learning and pedagogy have advanced enough to recognize the fallacy of this kind of weeding-out mentality! However, the advances do not mean that teachers do not still hold on to such erroneous thinking.

Protecting the "sanctity" of disciplines such as physics and chemistry, or math courses such as calculus, or even AP courses in all disciplines, creates a disenfranchising environment for learners who may have the interest and ability but may grasp concepts in nonlinear ways. Such an environment holds them to strict rules of behavior and demonstrations of their knowledge and understanding.

The connections between Dimension III/Protective and Dimension IV/Disenfranchising are unmistakable and must be understood within and apart from the curricular autonomy. Although not always the case, if not addressed, Protective IP can be a precursor to Disenfranchising IP. This is especially true in disciplines other than English and math, which are more likely to have more formalized curricula tied to annual assessments that provide schools, districts, and states with summative information on student progress. In English/language arts classes, we see such protective and disenfranchising behaviors when teachers hold fast to certain stories and books ("I have to teach this book because it's in the curriculum") even when their building leader has given them the green light to do otherwise. There is a feeling students must read a particular story or book or that students will love a book simply because the teacher does. Teachers may also use their power to explicitly message to students that their use of home and out-of-school languages have no place in school, as we saw with Amy's connection between speech and sounding "educated." In other disciplines, this dynamic may appear in more subtle ways.

Although the use of home language is not necessarily a primary issue in non-ELA classrooms, teachers in the disciplines are not exempt for enacting negative dimensions of the Power Principle in myriad ways. The following example offers insight into this situation.

Student Exclusion: A Case Study

Many years ago, I witnessed the use of student exclusion as a tool to protect teacher power and disenfranchise students. A student I will call Sheila had a science teacher I will call Ms. Thoms, a colleague of mine whom I highly respected for her deep content knowledge and what I thought was a genuine care for students. Ms. Thoms ran what can be called a tight ship. Her students knew the rules and knew they had very little leeway to move outside the established boundaries. One reason for these rules was because students worked on lab exercises with dangerous materials. Understandably, safety rules were necessary to ensure students would use chemicals and other materials and tools properly.

Ms. Thoms was one of those teachers who seemed to hold fast to the "every child can learn" mantra. However, upon close listening, her real beliefs about students would slip out in word and deed, especially when she spoke about students who were considered on grade level versus those considered above or below grade level. In the school where we worked, students could take algebra in 7th grade and geometry in 8th grade. Although this policy wasn't technically tracking, it mirrored tracking because all of the students who were in the algebra and geometry classes had the same block schedule, and their math and English classes were understood to be honors-level classes.

It was always apparent when Ms. Thoms's class contained more students from the so-called honors classes than students from the so-called on- or below-grade-level classes. She would share how enjoyable her class had been, how much work she had been able to complete, and how much better students had listened to her and followed her directions. She would be eager to share the successes of the students in these classes, especially when it came to the labs she had students complete.

After expressing her pleasure with this class, Ms. Thoms usually followed up with statements about what she was not looking forward to in her other classes. She would say things such as "These kids won't be able to handle my labs" or "These kids aren't prepared to do serious science work." Her language evidenced her underlying beliefs, which manifested in how she used her instructional power with the students in her on- and below-grade-level classes. This use of power was most evident with Sheila.

Being a typical middle schooler, Sheila was quite talkative and keenly aware of how teachers treated students. I had the pleasure and challenge of having Sheila in my class and learned a great deal about her struggles with other teachers, particularly Ms. Thoms. On those days when Ms. Thoms sent Sheila to my room, one of the first things Sheila typically would say was "Marshall, it wasn't me. I didn't do anything." At this point you may be chuckling because you've heard students say this very thing many times. But in Sheila's case, students would echo her sentiment and mention how Ms. Thoms would allow certain students to talk or give them a warning, but with Sheila and other students, she had no tolerance and would simply remove them from class.

The racial lines here have to be addressed because research has demonstrated the disproportionate discipline Black girls experience relative to their Asian and White classmates for matters like talking in class (Delpit, 1995; Monroe, 2005; Morris, 2016). I have not met a middle school girl who did not have to be reminded frequently to stop talking. The relevant point here is that Ms. Thoms is White, which further exacerbates the dynamic.

By removing Sheila from class, Ms. Thoms did a few things. First, she controlled the amount of science education Sheila received. Sheila's ability to make up missed work was at Ms. Thoms's discretion. Sometimes she allowed it; other times she did not. She also messaged to Sheila that her talking was more of an issue than it was for others who talked in class. Finally, Sheila learned that in order to be part of Ms. Thoms's class, she had to shelve her identity because her talking was viewed negatively, whereas that of other girls—largely White and part of the so-called honors group—was viewed as normal adolescent behavior. Sheila was measured against a different set of criteria.

As a student in my class, Sheila often asked questions—lots of questions. She was inquisitive, and when something came to her mind, her hand shot up. Additionally, she was eager to engage other students in dialogue—sometimes about the work and sometimes not.

On one particular occasion, Ms. Thoms called my room and asked if she could send Sheila down. I consented. When she came into my classroom, Sheila was near tears. She explained, "Ms. Marshall, all I did was try to ask a question. We was working on a lab, and there was something I didn't understand and I wanted to be sure I was doing what she asked. So I tried to ask her. She ignored me, and when one of the other girls asked the same question I had, she answered her. I got real mad and told her about herself. That's when she kicked me out."

Translation: Sheila had reached her boiling point with Ms. Thoms. After repeatedly being ignored, only to witness other girls—usually White and from the honors classes—get the attention they requested, it was time to make her anger known.

Sheila was in one of Ms. Thoms's classes with a number of students who were taking geometry in 8th grade. Like many students, Sheila could look around her core English and math classes and notice the difference in the student population, compared with the students in her science and social studies classes. She was capable but did not like math and did not test well enough on summative assessments to get placed in the algebra class in 7th grade, which meant she was automatically out of the 8th grade geometry class. Her schedule just happened to place her in science and social studies classes with many of the geometry students. Sheila knew the dynamics of Ms. Thoms's class. As she explained, it became clear that her questions would not be answered, and students who were not considered the smart kids had to wait or rely on their interpretation of the directions or content. Sheila was not afraid to advocate for her understanding.

Unfortunately, Ms. Thoms's use of power became a barrier to Sheila's understanding in the science class and was one of the reasons Sheila was sent to my classroom on numerous occasions. By sending Sheila out of the classroom, Ms. Thoms used her rightful authority to manage the classroom as she saw fit; however, her style disenfranchised students like Sheila. Considering the number of days of possible instruction and the fact that Sheila was removed from class at least twice per month, she was deprived of at least 20 days of science instruction during the school year as punishment for speaking up for herself and challenging the inequitable environment she faced. Again, the suggestion here is not that Ms. Thoms did not have the authority to manage her classroom. It is that she did not have the right to undereducate students as part of her classroom management strategies. Because Ms. Thoms was a respected member of the team with many years of experience, her own colleagues—myself included—were reluctant to confront the behavior many of us knew to be harmful to students.

The teacher-student relationship is ripe for misuse of adult power. We see here how it can deprive students of their right to a high-quality education. We see how in certain environments teachers require students to conform to a set of norms that serve the teacher instead of being an authentic partnership between teacher and learner. Students like Sheila will always be at a disadvantage in classrooms where a teacher believes only the identified "smart" students or students who observe the cultural norms the teacher identifies with and holds valid deserve to have their expression respected and their questions addressed. Although we can champion the need for students to develop learner independence, we can also admit it must not come in the form of students knowing they are unwelcomed because the adult in the room uses removal from the classroom as the first line of defense against them. We can see how so-called honors classrooms can be catalysts for student exclusion, as teachers protect their beliefs about the sanctity of leveled classrooms, especially those designated as honors. It is important to note, however, that similar situations occur in classes of all levels.

Howard (2016) has stated that teachers quietly believe students fall into one of four buckets related to their intellect: smart, somewhat smart, not very smart, and dumb. In the case we just explored, it is not clear whether Ms. Thoms believed Sheila belonged to the "not very smart" or the "dumb" bucket; we just know she did not classify Sheila as "smart." The value system and the hidden curriculum were clear. Ms. Thoms valued students who were either in the higher-level classes or compliant. The hidden curriculum held that students were measured against their adherence to her ideology of smartness. You had to be in the honors classes to be valued and to have the right to advocate for yourself.

The Case Study: A Different Approach

Taking Ms. Thoms as our test case, let's consider how she might have used her instructional power differently to evidence a different set of beliefs and provide support for her students. Here are some possibilities.

The use of phrases such as "these students" is usually a signal of deficit thinking. To move beyond this, Ms. Thoms would need to examine her belief system about her students and make a concerted effort to recognize when she was engaging in such thinking. She could do this in many ways, including the following:

- Be courageous enough to record audio of herself so she could hear her own words and then reflect on whether they reflect her true beliefs.
- Conduct an analysis of when she is most likely to remove students from class and the lessons being taught at the time. Such an examination could highlight the need to differentiate instruction to better meet her students' interests and academic needs.

Sheila's statement "I got real mad and told her about herself" could have been a signal that something needed to change. It presented an opportunity for Ms. Thoms to learn, which could have been approached in various ways, including the following:

- Invite Sheila to a one-on-one conference to better understand why she reacted the way she did. This would require Ms. Thoms to enter the conversation from a learning stance and not a reprimanding stance.
- Invite a colleague to videotape her class so she could see it from the students' perspective.
- Use a system to ensure she engages more students in the learning. Many teachers use name cards, popsicle sticks, marbles, and other tools, and once they call on a student, they place the object in a box, move the card to the back of a pile, and so forth, as a way to avoid calling on that student until others have been given an opportunity to share.

‖ PAUSE TO REFLECT

What Might Be Causing a Strained Relationship with a Student?

Consider a student with whom you may be having a strained relationship. Answer the following questions to understand the possible causes:

- How are you using your words either in front of students or with your colleagues?
- Are you using the dreaded phrase "these kids" or other terminology that signals an unrecognized deficit perspective?
- Are you using your power to reduce students' instructional opportunities? If so, how, specifically? ▶

If your answers to the reflection questions reveal problems with a particular student, consider inviting the student to a sit-down session to figure how to move toward a more positive relationship. By taking the time to examine your words and actions, you might uncover some hidden deficits that are hindering student success.

Looking Ahead

In this chapter, we explored how words and actions reveal the principles guiding decision making. The next chapter provides more opportunities to think about and improve your practice. The journey continues.

5 | THE DYNAMIC MATRIX: CONSIDERING WHERE YOU LAND

Man, know thyself.

— *African Proverb*

Although the above quote has been attributed to Greek philosophers, it originated on the African continent. Self-knowledge is the crux of this chapter. Moving toward building empowering and agentive learning environments for your students begins with you knowing yourself and where you are on this important journey.

Now that we've laid the foundation for your understanding of the Power Principle matrix and how it works across disciplines, it's time to further unpack your practice through the lens of your curricular autonomy and the dimensions of power that shape your instructional decision making.

Understanding the dynamic nature of the matrix is perhaps the most important element of determining how you use your instructional power. Remember those 1,500 decisions you make in a given day? Each one of those is what I call "3 × 3 = 9" decisions. If I were to ask you, "What's 3 × 3?" you would quickly and correctly respond with "9." Although your brain goes through the usual machinations of processing questions and coming up with correct answers, getting to 9 is not something you consciously think about; you respond automatically, almost as soon as the question is posed.

The same is true with many of the instructional decisions you make. You've made so many, so often, it is hard to stop and think about what lies behind the decisions you've made or even those you are about to make. You're in 3 × 3 = 9 mode.

Kicking the tires of your instructional decision making using the lens of the Power Principle matrix allows you to slow down and consider how students are affected by your decisions. Attending to the components of your instructional practice (e.g., your identity, your classroom culture, your disposition) is necessary to ensure you are creating the type of environment where students know they are valued, can achieve academic and social success, and do not have to conform to ways of being that indicate that who they are must be shelved in order to fit a prescribed mold.

As noted earlier, it is easy to make assumptions about the relationship between curricular autonomy and the dimensions of instructional power. Given the dynamic nature of teaching and learning, such assumptions are unproductive; they rob us of the ability to deeply reflect on our practice and to understand how children are affected.

Early in my teaching career, I taught middle school social studies. It was the first time I had taught anything other than English language arts. I was on a team where the tenured teacher got first dibs to choose a discipline, and as the newcomer on the team, I was assigned social studies. Because the subject was not included in the state assessment, I had a lot of curricular autonomy, and the content was not prescriptive. I had a mix of Calibrated and Unfettered Curricular Autonomy. It was calibrated because the district provided the textbook and many of my instructional materials, but I was not mandated to follow them. I could choose materials outside those provided, and no one checked whether what I was teaching aligned to social studies standards. I was free to make the types of curricular decisions I thought would best meet my students' needs.

At the time, I would be considered an "old school" educator. Although I never believed in the "sit and get" approach to instruction, I did believe in having very clear boundaries between me and my students. My expectations were high, and students knew it. I liked to say I pulled out of my students what they did not even know was in them to give or produce. In having calibrated autonomy and a welcoming classroom environment where my students knew I believed in them, I could examine my practices and recognize instances where I worked to protect my position as the leader with the most knowledge in the class. I developed my own assessments, which were legendary, and I went to great lengths to make them as cheat-proof as possible, creating multiple versions within and across classes. Because social studies was not assessed at the state level, I had full control over assessments; the district just wanted to be sure content was assessed. This freedom was another aspect of the calibrated autonomy I enjoyed.

I was particularly proud of my assessment for a unit on the Babylonian empire. It had all the testing bells and whistles: multiple-choice, true/false, and open-ended questions and two essays. I provided students with possible essay topics beforehand, and I allowed them to have note cards for the essay section, but the notes could only contain bullet items, not full sentences. Students had 90 minutes to complete the test.

I had an exceptional student, whom I will call Marian, who worked extremely hard in everything she did. As I read through Marian's test, I realized she was getting *every* answer correct, and her essay demonstrated a high level of content mastery on the rise and fall of the Babylonian empire. She was about to get a perfect score of *100*, but I could not allow that to happen. There had to be some way I could deduct at least one point! After all, no student had earned a *100* on any assessment of mine.

So what did I do? I searched Marian's test until I found a tiny error that would justify deducting one point from her score. She had spelled one word incorrectly. Whew! I was saved. I had found something to protect my reputation as a hard tester. I had used my grading power to protect my position, and in so doing, I robbed Marian of something precious.

After that assessment, Marian's mom scheduled a conference with me. In that conference, I learned Marian considered me one of her favorite teachers. She had shared with her mother how appreciative she was of having a teacher who held students to high academic standards. Her mother also shared how hard Marian had prepared for the test and how seeing the score of *99* was devastating because the one-point deduction was for something so minor. Marian's mom did not ask me to change her daughter's grade, but she did let me know I had missed an opportunity to show Marian the importance of having high expectations without forcing perfection.

I reached out to Marian and talked with her about her feelings. Although she was cordial and respectful, I saw the light go out of her eyes. She remained a stellar student in my class, but my need for perfection for my own protection had dimmed her light. Marian did not participate as she once had. She was more reserved and would not engage with me as she had before that test. My need to protect myself caused irreparable damage to our relationship.

Now, this may not be your story. I was unaware of my power at the time and simply thought I was doing the right thing. After all, I was an effective teacher; my students left my class with solid content knowledge as well as strong literacy skills. Unfortunately, my instructional power fell within the Protective dimension of the Power Principle matrix, and my strategies created situations in which students' best efforts would still not be good enough. My pushing them to achieve perfection became a deterrent. The overall classroom environment was positive, and students had opportunities to demonstrate knowledge in a variety of ways and to share ideas about how they would like to engage in learning.

Despite the positive aspects of my class, a hidden curriculum held students to an impossible bar. They were held to something I had lacked. As an African American student, I went to predominantly White schools with all White teachers. My teachers could have been the evidence for research about how White teachers see their Black students. They were always nice and always made an effort to include me in the social aspects of the class. However, high academic expectations were reserved for the other students—students who did not look like me.

Once I decided to become an educator, I made it my mission to have high expectations for every child I had the opportunity to teach. Unfortunately, I had not reflected on the implications of the way I executed my expectations. Thinking about this through the lens of the Power Principle matrix, I was the teacher with high measures of autonomy; but in some ways, I used that power to protect my position as the intellectual leader of the class. High expectations became a double-edged sword used against students if they did not perform up to my standards against a hidden curriculum they knew nothing about.

Teachers are often expected to disembody themselves once they step into the classroom, and many teachers make a valiant attempt to do so. However, when you leave your home, you take your full self with you. No part of you is left in the car only to be picked up once school ends. All aspects of your beliefs, ideologies, history, and worldview go with you. It was not until I took time to reflect on the incident with Marian that I realized I had been enacting a protective pedagogy with my students, and if I did not address the situation, it would devolve into a disenfranchising pedagogy. I took my personal history of teachers having low expectations of me and went in the opposite direction with my students. On the surface, doing so seemed like a good thing. What I did not realize then was the harm it was inflicting on the psyche of my students. It was creating anxiety as they tried to reach my bar only to learn that each time they got close, I moved the bar higher.

This experience became part of my view of education. Every child deserves a teacher who believes in their ability to have academic success. I believed this while I was in the classroom, and I believe it today. What I had to learn was the existence of a fine line between my expectations and the potential for those expectations to become a hammer against my students instead of a tool to support them.

As noted, I enjoyed a high level of curricular autonomy, and for the most part, my classroom would have fallen into Dimension II/Agentive instructional power. My students and I engaged in lively exchanges about the curriculum I presented. I often sought their ideas about how best to approach their understanding. On top of challenging assessments, I gave them projects designed to reflect as much of their personalities and interests as they desired. And yet, I still held on to elements of Dimension III/Protective power, which veered into Dimension IV/Disenfranchising power. My story demonstrates the dynamism within the Power Principle matrix and the importance of deeply understanding ourselves as people so we can better understand how who we are and what we carry with us shape how we make instructional decisions.

Now that you've read my story, it's time for you to reflect on your own educational legacy. What might be the underpinnings of your teaching life that could be shaping a hidden curriculum in your classroom? What parts of your learning legacy are creating the most dynamism in your power-laden instructional decisions?

You began this work in Chapter 2, where you were asked to consider how values were communicated by your home and school environments. Now you're going to go a step further and look under the hood of your teaching by creating your own case study. This exercise will give you deeper insight into how you approach instructional decisions and what might be the driving force behind them. By creating your own case study, you can learn about the ways in which you cross power dimensions in the Power Principle matrix.

Bishop (1990) talked about the importance of students having windows and mirrors in the literature they encounter. This wonderful concept is meant to urge educators to give students of color more opportunities to read literature that features characters like them, so they can see themselves on the pages of the stories and books they read. I'm extending the "doors and mirrors" metaphor to the exercises in this chapter. It's easier to look out of doors than to look into mirrors; however, far too many children are suffering at the hands of educators who spend more time looking outward than they do looking inward. My goal is for you to be one of those who reverse this practice. Taking more time to look inward will give you the data you need to ensure that what you think you see in your classroom is actually there.

Case Study: A Self-Analysis Exercise

Choose two classes: one in which you believe you are more often at your best and the other in which you know there are challenges. Begin with the challenging class, and then repeat the analysis using the other class. Starting with the challenging class will make the task easier because you will be on the lookout for the places where you may be in the Protective or Disenfranchising dimensions of instructional power.

Step 1: Answer the Following Foundational Questions

- If you teach multiple grades, what grade are you using to build this portion of your case study?

- If you teach multiple disciplines, what discipline are you using to build this portion of your case study?
- If you teach a single grade and a single discipline, what class period are you using to build this portion of your case study?

Step 2: Conduct a Demographic Analysis of Your Case Class Using the Following Categories

- Gender
  - Number of boys
  - Number of girls
  - Number of transgender boys, if you have definitive knowledge
  - Number of transgender girls, if you have definitive knowledge
  - Number of nonbinary students, if you have definitive knowledge
- Race/ethnicity *(Note: Race and ethnicity are complex concepts to define and categorize. Use your best judgment and prioritize how students choose to identify.)*
  - African American/Black
  - American Indian/Indigenous
  - Arab or Arab American
  - Asian/Asian American
  - Biracial
  - Hispanic/Latinx
  - Multiethnic
  - Multiracial
  - Pacific Islander
  - White/European descended
- Religion
  - How do students identify their religious affiliation?
- Sexual orientation (Be careful in getting answers for this component.)
  - Bisexual
  - Female
  - Male
  - Nonbinary

- Economic situation
  - Number of students who receive assistance via FaRM (Free and/or Reduced Meals)
  - Number of students who do not receive assistance via FaRM
- Academic level
  - Number/percent of students considered above grade level
  - Number/percent of students considered on grade level
  - Number/percent of students considered below grade level
  - Number/percent of students receiving academic support via special education services IEPs, 504s
  - Number/percent of students becoming multilingual via English learning

Step 3: Conduct a Qualitative Analysis

For this section of your case study, you may choose to focus on a single element (like my grading incident) or something broader. The analysis is more important than the choice. Your willingness to look in your mirror and honestly evaluate your decisions is the most important factor. Here are some options for you to consider.

Option 1: Building relationships. How do you build relationships with your students? Be explicit and think carefully about the steps you take to connect with them. Language is often not considered a part of relationship building; however, how we use words reveals the underlying belief systems that show up in our actions. You will need to carefully consider your use of language to get at what may be driving your relationship dynamics. Doing so may be a challenge because it is difficult to analyze something that feels so natural.

Use the following prompts to guide your thinking about how you build relationships:

- Consider the students with whom you found it easier to build relationships. What made it easier? Were there similarities in demographic factors? Interests? Personality traits? Did you use language the same way? (Remember the examples of Erin and Beth. Culturally dynamic language was critical to their relationships with their students.) Now consider the students with whom you have a tenuous relationship or where building a relationship did not come easily. What made it challenging? Demographics? Interests? Personality? Again, try to pinpoint the elements that made building the relationship challenging.

- Think back to your own schooling. Which teachers were you closest to? Why? How did the relationship develop? What did your teachers do to foster a relationship with you? What role did you play in the relationship-building process? Which teachers did you struggle to connect to? Why? What did these teachers do that may have been barriers to your ability to develop a positive relationship with them? What was your role in the relationship challenge?

- For those relationships you have found to be challenging, lean into yourself and not on your students. What hidden layers within yourself make relationship building easier with some students and challenging with others? What hidden curriculum might you be holding students to that is affecting your ability to build strong relationships with all of them? You may think you are being neutral; however, students are very aware of who you favor and who you simply tolerate. Your words and actions convey your beliefs. What are the subtle ways you may be signaling this to students? What is the hidden reward system (getting called on more, having more opportunities for sharing, getting more of your time) that students may be vying for in their quest to build a relationship with you? What are you learning about yourself from the students who do not participate in the process?

Option 2: Classroom management. Review your class management structure. Use the following prompts as a guide:

- How do you use language to manage your classroom? Do you use directive or suggestive speech? How does your tone affect student reactions to you? How would your students characterize your tone? Is speech correction part of your management repertoire? (Remember the example of Amy.)
- If your walls could speak, what would they say? What is the prevailing message students are receiving about their place in your classroom relative to your place in the classroom? You may have clear boundaries; however, consider the messaging. What posters do you have in your room? What beliefs do they convey? How are they conveying your beliefs about students, education, learning, and other factors? What was most effective about the way you communicated your boundaries?
- What is the hidden curriculum of your classroom management legacy? How were classes managed when you were in school? How are students being judged and held accountable, and perhaps suffering the consequences of a legacy about which they have no knowledge? Do you have a hidden reward system?

Option 3: Grading. Review your grading policies. How are students graded? What hidden factors are driving your grading decisions? The following prompts can help you evaluate your approach to grading:

- Choose several student work samples from across your demographic profile. Copy the samples and remove student names. Review your grading criteria, and then regrade the student work. Compare your grading of the unnamed samples against the original grades the students received. Were there differences? Did you give or deduct points for items or information not expressly contained in your grading criteria?
- Do you grade students on "soft" measures (i.e., moving through the hallways in silence, students bringing in school supplies, hav-

ing notes signed by parents/guardians)? What values are communicated through your grading?

- Do you see evidence of your own grading legacy—how you may have earned grades in school—in your practice? Is this part of a hidden reward system not shared with students?

Option 4: The power of the referral pen. Research has demonstrated disciplinary disparities by race and gender. Use the following prompts to consider how you use your school's referral system:

- Review your discipline data for the classes you've chosen to analyze. When are you most likely to threaten the use of referral? When are you most likely to remove a student from class without a referral? When are you most likely to refer a student for administrative disciplinary action? What are the primary reasons for which you have chosen to discipline a student formally or informally? Which students have not been disciplined formally or informally?
- What differences do you notice between the classes you've analyzed? Is there evidence of a hidden reward system?
- Think back to when you were a student. How does your use of discipline compare to what you remember experiencing or observing?
- What do the reasons for which you choose to discipline students communicate about your beliefs? How are students being held to your underlying beliefs about the relationship between adults and students? What is the hidden curriculum against which students are being held accountable?

Locating Your Case Study Within the Power Principle Matrix

Now that you've constructed your personal case study, it's time to determine what it reveals about your location in the Power Principle matrix. The instructional decisions you have been making are filtered through a legacy of your schooling experiences, which you may not have considered until now. The combination of this (perhaps unrecognized) legacy, your educational ideologies, and the various dynamics of power is a complicated puzzle. Taking time to disentangle these structures can help ensure that your approach to the various students you teach is as free of prejudice and bias as possible. Let's use my case study involving Marian as the model.

According to the characteristics of the four quadrants of the Power Principle matrix, I would be somewhere between Dimension II/Agentive and Dimension III/Protective. A case could also be made for me venturing into Dimension IV/Disenfranchising. Let's dig in and see where I might actually land.

We'll begin with curricular autonomy. The district in my case study considered itself progressive and did not expressly dictate the curriculum. Teachers assessed students regularly; however, state summative assessments were not the driving force behind our curricular or instructional decisions. We had the latitude to focus on the content and strong instruction so our students would be prepared for their next grade. The district was racially, ethnically, and economically diverse and was generally considered high performing. We had students who received free and reduced meals and students who received special education services. We did not, however, have a large population of students who were becoming multilingual through English learning. Based on these characteristics, I enjoyed Calibrated Curricular Autonomy. I received curricular guidance—I had to check in with my principal at least twice a month to review my instructional plans and teaching—but there were no express curricular or instructional mandates.

There are three areas shaping the components of the power dimensions: beliefs, environment/culture, and grading. We'll work through each one as we look inside my practice.

Beginning with beliefs, I sat squarely between Dimension II/Agentive and Dimension III/Protective. I believed—and continue to

believe—in the intellectual capacity of every child. I structured learning around students' interests and worked to help them understand
the importance of self-advocacy, especially regarding the need to
advocate for academic support. However, despite these underlying
beliefs, I still held on to what could be called traditional beliefs about
the relationship boundaries adults and children should observe.
Although my students and I worked on classroom rules together, I
had drafted them before seeking any student input. The process was
more about having them weigh in on the boundaries I had established
by collaborating with their peers to come up with examples of the
behaviors that fit under the categories I provided. I also gave students
the opportunity to determine appropriate consequences. However, I
shaped the starting point of the classroom management process. As
the adult, I believed it was my responsibility to structure the learning,
and I had the final say on the operational aspects of the class. This
ideology was driven by my own upbringing and educational histories.
Based on classroom management aspects of my teaching, I operated
in Dimension III/Protective.

Nevertheless, other aspects of my teaching revealed a more agentive than protective approach. Culturally, I fostered an environment
in which my students and I collaborated a great deal on how they
would represent their learning. Because I grew up in a household
where we could negotiate for certain things and I had experienced a
lot of leadership in my religious upbringing, I valued student voice. I
also understood the need to help students learn and practice how to
exercise their voice. I encouraged them to question, challenge, and
offer ideas about how they should engage with content. They learned
how to use their agency in advocating for the assistance they needed
to complete their work. Although developing student agency had not
been part of my educational history, I had had enough experiences
in other areas of my life to appreciate the value of instilling young
people with a sense of the importance of their voice.

Culturally, the classroom was lively, with positive peer-to-peer and teacher-to-student relationships. Students knew they were valued, and there was evidence they enjoyed class, despite the heavy workload and what some described as "hard stuff to do."

Admittedly, however, I had a hidden curriculum of perfection against which students were held. This shaped my actions and put me between Dimension III/Protective and Dimension IV/Disenfranchising. I took pride in being the teacher that students knew would require them to use every ounce of their intellect to be successful. My students knew I would push them to think deeply and produce high-quality work.

This belief system had its advantages and disadvantages. When students saw my name on their schedule, their friends would say, "Oh. You got Ms. Marshall." The reaction carried a heavy weight as students anticipated the year ahead. I took great care to develop learning experiences to ensure students would be engaged, but I also had a running dialogue in my head about whether the task met my high standards of rigor. There's pride and then there's *pride*. I took positive pride in my ability to get students to think critically about a wide range of topics and my ability to get them to believe in themselves enough to commit to the type of work I was asking them to do. But I also worked to protect a reputation that went beyond being a skilled practitioner. Here, I fell between the Agentive and Protective dimensions of power.

My Dimension III/Protective leaning morphed into Dimension IV/Disenfranchising when it came to grading. As I shared in my account about Marian, I was not going to let a child get a perfect score on one of my assessments, because doing so would send a message to students that perhaps it was an easy thing to accomplish. It did not occur to me to think about the amount of studying Marian might have done. Because I had been subject to a perfectionist model of education (which, in reflection, I believe was actually tied to low expectations—an observation I'll explain shortly), I held my students to the same level; doing so was part of my hidden curriculum. Looking for the slightest error in Marian's test protected the sanctity of my own perceptions of rigor. By deducting the requisite point, I saved myself from her perfect score. But in so doing, I disenfranchised her and sent the message that no matter how hard she worked, perfection was out of reach.

Such stringency creates stress and anxiety as students work overtime to meet impossible expectations that are couched as having high expectations. My behavior went beyond expecting students to achieve their best; it held them to a hidden curriculum I believed was necessary to ensure that my reputation as the most rigorous teacher remained intact. Clearly my behavior fell into the Dimension IV/Disenfranchising quadrant of the Power Principle matrix. After giving Marian a *99* instead of the *100* she had earned, I felt better—but at the expense of her sense of accomplishment and well-being. Although she remained a top performer, she showed an almost imperceptible shift in how she participated in class, as evidenced during a review of a rubric for an upcoming project.

As was our usual practice, students were allowed to meet with self-selected partners or work independently to make sense of the project specs and the rubric. After the allotted time for independent review ended, I brought the class together to take clarifying questions. Several students asked questions about timeframes and possible products, but no one asked about content. I asked the class if anyone had questions about the content or grading, to which Marian replied, "Does it really matter if we have questions about grading?" Although her classmates did not know where her uncharacteristically bold question came from, I certainly did. She was letting me know that she no longer trusted me to fairly assess student work. I was on notice. I had won the power game, but Marian let me know it was a hollow win, resulting from my decision to exercise my grading power in ways that protected me while harming her. This example illustrates the crux of how Dimensions III and IV work. Needless to say, the incident caused me a lot of consternation and regret, but I am tremendously grateful for the experience because it forced me to consider my ideologies, disposition, and actions.

Figure 5.1 shows how I would portray my story in the Power Principle matrix. Because my district allowed measures of curricular autonomy, I situated myself in the Calibrated category of curricular autonomy. My need to hold students to rigid rules and protect what I believed was my intellectual superiority placed me in Dimension

FIGURE 5.1

Sample Portrayal of the Power Principle at Work

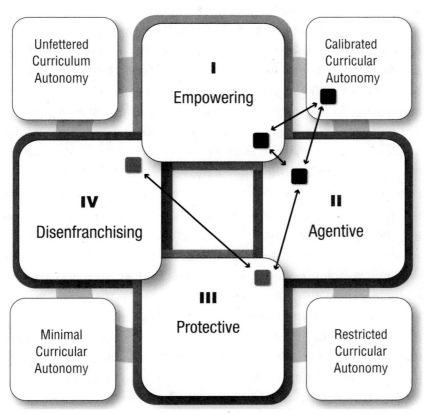

III/Protective instructional power, but my grading of Marian was evidence of being in Dimension IV/Disenfranchising. At the same time, I showed elements of Dimension II/Agentive as I worked with my students to share some of the classroom responsibilities. As an educator who really believed I was doing what was right for and by children, I used my instructional power in dynamic ways, revealing what I believe is a familiar story.

Unearthing the Roots of the Power Dimensions

I firmly believe no teacher consciously sets out to be a protective or disenfranchising educator. To a large extent, we slip into these dimensions because we live unexamined professional lives. The brain, although highly complex, likes routine and actually fights against laying down new ones. Consider this example. One morning, my husband had to drive our daughter to her sitter, breaking our normal routine of my doing this particular task. Instead of driving her to the sitter, he inadvertently began following his typical routine and driving to work. It wasn't until our 5-year-old asked where she was going that he realized what was happening. We've all had similar incidents, where we've had to break our routine only to find ourselves defaulting back to it without much thought. Call it the brain's comfort zone. Because we make so many new decisions throughout the day, the brain likes to leave space for those by not having to think about the ones it knows by heart.

Not being fully conscious of the impact of your automatic decision-making processes can both build students up and inadvertently tear them down. It can subject them to ideas that you have long forgotten but that still shape how you think about and interact with students, and it can affect how and when you access your highest ability to educate them. For instance, we see abysmal national outcomes in reading and math for many students of color, especially African American students. School is the place where group disparities begin to widen, and the longer certain groups of students stay in school, the more the arc of their skill development flattens (Wexler, 2020). A common belief says that Black and Hispanic/Latina/o/x children are not especially good at math and science. Plus, enrollment numbers in math and science courses display disproportionalities, and teachers and administrators make it an issue solely of student unprepared-ness instead of understanding how the dimensions of power have shaped access to the courses students need to advance academically (Stambaugh & Ford, 2014; Toldson, 2019). The low expectations about aptitude, exacerbated by structural barriers, become the "3 × 3 = 9" way in which we think about groups of students instead of taking the time to learn more about them. Furthermore, although the academic expectations for Black and Hispanic/Latina/o/x children are low, the expectations for their adherence to rules and regulations are high. Just look at the discipline rates at any school and you will see the disparities. Black students face harsher and more frequent instances of referrals, suspensions, and other disciplinary actions than their White counterparts for the same offenses. These realities reflect power-laden decisions that adversely affect certain students while benefitting others.

Unexplored and unresolved educational histories affect teachers' current use of instructional power. The dimensions defy discipline and must be understood through the lens of how students experience learning in the classroom. It is important to ask yourself whether or not you are creating space for yourself to examine your educational history to get at the root of your use of power as it relates to your curricular autonomy.

You've walked with me through my excavation process. You've seen where I landed across the matrix and learned about the educational history that laid the foundation for how I used my instructional power. Now it's your turn to do some digging to uncover where you may be on the Power Principle matrix and what may be the under-lying factors that led you there (see Figure 5.2). Responding to the

FIGURE 5.2

Examining Your Educational History and Its Impacts

Reflection	Response	Impact on Your Teaching	Hidden or Explicit
Your Educational History			
Identify an event during your educational experience as a student that had the greatest positive influence on your educational philosophy. What role did the teacher's language play in making the event memorable?			
Identify an event during your educational experience as a student that had the greatest negative influence on your educational philosophy. What role did the teacher's language play in making the event negative?			
Enacting Your Educational History			
Identify an event during your teaching experience that most exemplified the positive aspects of your educational history. How might your language use have affected the experience?		How did you enact this part of your history? (Words/Actions) What triggered this reaction?	

Reflection	Response	Impact on Your Teaching	Hidden or Explicit
Enacting Your Educational History			
Identify an event during your teaching experience that most exemplified the negative aspects of your educational history.		How did you enact this part of your history? (Words/Actions)	
How might your use of language have affected the experience?		What triggered this reaction?	

Based on your responses, where do you place yourself on the Power Principle matrix?

What types of student actions/words are most likely to trigger the positive aspects of your educational history?

What types of student actions/words are most likely to trigger the negative aspects of your educational history?

prompts and questions in Figure 5.2 may be a challenge, but your results provide the opportunity to look closely into your mirror and more fully understand the triggers that could be leading to behaviors that disenfranchise students.

Moving Between Dimensions on the Matrix

Now let's explore how to move between dimensions. We'll use my original case study as a guide.

Remember, my curricular autonomy was calibrated, and I landed in Dimension III/Protective and Dimension IV/Disenfranchising as I chose to grade Marian's work in a way that ensured I maintained my reputation as a tough teacher. After reflecting on the situation, here's how I made changes to my instructional perspective and practices.

First, I took stock of why I needed to be what was called a "tough" teacher. I challenged myself to engage in the following reflective activity by addressing these questions:

For whom am I teaching? Answering this question was the biggest challenge. The easy answer was to say to myself I was teaching for the kids, of course. But when I stopped to consider the decisions I was making, I realized my style of teaching was about crafting a teaching persona I thought was necessary to garner respect from my students. My mindset was "It is better to be respected than liked." Sure, my students eventually grew to like me, but only after they understood I was there to get them to learn; we'd deal with whether or not they liked me along the way.

How is my teaching persona affecting students? This question was trickier for me to fully understand. My students were fully engaged, completed assignments, performed well on my assessments and the district assessments, and the overall culture of the classes appeared positive. I knew my students had strong relationships with my colleagues, so I challenged myself to see if there was any student talk about my class and, more important, about me. I pointedly asked people if they had heard anything from students about how my class was going. What I learned was revelatory. My colleagues shared that my students did enjoy my class because it was challenging, but they found me hard to get to know because I seemed closed to them. I even had a parent tell me her son enjoyed my class very much because it was the first time in his schooling that he felt challenged. Yeah! Unfortunately, she added that her son also believed my expectations sometimes seemed impossible to meet because I appeared unreachable. This revelation was definitely a hard pill to swallow. I had come to education from retail, where the bottom line was most important. Taking this approach into my teaching had been effective from a bottom-line perspective, but I was unsuccessful on measures my students found most important.

What specific changes are needed? I had a choice: stay my course and keep pushing my students while ignoring the affective domain, or find a way to incorporate both. Here's what I did:

- I focused on two domains of my class: the affective and the cognitive. Affectively, I chose to let my students know more about who I was as a person, making myself more available to those who needed extra help, and leading an after-school club so I could get to know my students outside the classroom. I also invited my students to help me learn more about them by incorporating reflective questions into my lessons to get at both the cognitive and affective elements of their learning.
- Cognitively, I restructured my assignments to give students more flexibility in how they demonstrated their knowledge and understanding. I allowed them to choose work partners and elements of their assessments. The move toward student choice in work partners began with an opening discussion about what makes an effective partner and collaborator. This introduction helped my students make better decisions about choosing part-

ners, and it also challenged students who tended not to be such great partners.

- I worked to be more culturally responsive to my students by soliciting specific examples of how our learning connected to their experiences as young people. I used reflective assignments after students completed work to learn from them how to make lessons more engaging as well to better understand how they were progressing.

What are the effects of my changes? I wanted to be sure what I was doing had positive effects. Although I did not go back to my colleagues to see how my students were registering any changes, I took inventory of what I saw happening. For starters, I was more relaxed, both physically and mentally. I felt as though giving myself permission to be more connected to my students was freeing. It allowed me to reduce some of the pressure I had been harboring to be perfect. I realized that perfectionism was robbing me of my ability to be authentic. Second, I saw a demonstrative change in my students. There were always students who participated in class, but as I changed, I noticed more student participation. The increased participation signaled a shift in culture and helped me better understand what my students needed. Moving in this direction gave me the ability to move toward the Empowering dimension.

Taking this inventory enabled me to come to terms with who I was as a teacher by considering why I made the decisions I did. Being a student of myself pushed me to be a better student of my students. I was able to move out of the Disenfranchising and Protective dimensions of instructional power toward the Agentive dimension. It took me some time to get fully into the Empowering dimension, because asking myself these questions was my first step in the process of self-discovery. I did not have the language of the Power Principle framework, so I had to do a lot of learning before I could become the balanced educator I knew I needed to be for my students.

Looking Ahead

In Chapter 6, we're going to discuss the Protective dimension in more depth. Protective instructional power in particular can be tricky to determine as the characteristics can be masked by other behaviors. As before, the journey continues.

6 | THE PROTECTIVE DIMENSION: A CLOSER LOOK

Education is the instrument of democratic designs. And it is no less the instrument of power. The control of information, the shaping of understanding, and the influence of judgment are critical elements common to democratic design, power theory, and educational philosophy.

— David Nyberg, "A Concept of Power for Education"

I recently reread one of my favorite books on education: *Education and Power*, by Michael Apple (1982). I've read it so many times, the pages are separating from the binding and turning yellow. Apple uses the phrase "black box" to describe the hidden aspects of schooling. We know black boxes hold critical information about the inner workings of airplane cockpits and are often used to determine the cause of malfunctions or other serious incidents (Bonsor & Chandler, 2001).

Education researchers use this phrase as a metaphor to describe the inner workings of entire educational processes and systems. In this chapter, I'll apply it to walk you through understanding those areas of your teaching that you need to uncover to get past your power-protecting tendencies.

I had to do some research on the black boxes found on airplanes to make sure I was applying the metaphor correctly. Here's what I learned. Black boxes are located in the back of the plane, not the cockpit; they are always on and capture *everything* about the mechanical workings of an airplane flight up to about 25 hours, from flight patterns to conversations among pilots and with air traffic controllers. The black box is the ultimate information-gathering device.

Imagine having a black box in your classroom, with your every pedagogical move recorded. Imagine being able to see so deeply into your teaching as to understand the inner workings of your decision-making processes. Throughout this book, we've been working to unlock your black box to get inside your teaching. In this chapter, we're going further to uncover the reasons and ways you may be engaging Dimension III/Protective power.

What Are You Protecting?

The domain of protection encompasses two categories: the schooling institution and the educator position. In maintaining societal structures, teachers work in schools to develop the academic capability of students while simultaneously ensuring young people are prepared to enter a preexisting sociocultural economic system. The degree to which students partner with their teachers in moving within the structures of the system is the degree to which students are rewarded or punished; afforded access to the spoils of education; or constrained, removed, or held back. When students cooperate with the system and fall in line with the schooling process, teachers have no need to use protective measures to get them back in line with the expectations of how they should comport themselves. Conversely, when students differ from the expected norm or they do not demonstrate it at all, there are consequences.

Protecting the System

As we've noted before, school is the primary vehicle through which children learn about society and its values. These values are built on a set of beliefs and ideologies that educators both protect and evidence. Like society, the system and process of schooling sorts children into groups. It is structured to maintain the rungs of society and ensure there are people ready and able to contribute various skills to guarantee a functioning society. Although many Americans believe in the myth of upward mobility, studies have shown that societies operate in ways that maintain their structural foundations (Delgado, 2007; McNamee & Miller, 2004). Upward mobility is quite difficult by design, and societies get the result they are structured to get—that is, stratification.

Schooling is part of this structure, and educators protect and evidence the system in how they use their instructional power. Spend a day in any school and you will see society's beliefs about the people it serves. Everything about the school will demonstrate the underlying ideologies about the students and their families. The school's structures and the behaviors of the adults who work in it will demonstrate society's expectations for those in attendance.

In considering how schools work to prepare students for society, we must consider how the process advances. On the surface, it is a noble undertaking to choose a job whose purpose is to prepare people to join society equipped with a set of acceptable skills. Every society needs citizens prepared for entry into its structure. Of course, students must learn how to interact with their peers and the adults around them. They need to learn how to manage their emotions, needs, and inclinations. And yes, they need to graduate from a school system (public, private, or charter, etc.) knowing more information and being able to do more than when they entered. What they do *not* need is to be sorted upon entry and conveyed through whatever system they attend for 12 years. They do not need to be made to believe that who they are is deficient simply because they do not conform with the societal demands schooling places upon them. The sorting mechanism of school is a primary part of what teachers protect when they enact their instructional power. Teachers protect and evidence the system by using their instructional power to perpetuate or disrupt systems.

What does it mean, then, for students to fit within the system of schooling? Although this question has no definitive answer, there are some processes we can point to for insight to help understand the "fix them" strategies many teachers use to protect the system and ensure students remain within its confines, including putting constraints on behavior, expression, and language use. Consider the following case.

The parents of a student I'll call Mario asked me to attend a parent-teacher conference to discuss some disturbing issues going on in her son's kindergarten class. Their 5-year-old had entered kindergarten "school ready." They had begun building his literacy and numeracy skills through reading, counting, and various other activities since he was a toddler. They read to him on a regular basis and involved him in household activities to foster a curiosity about the world around him. He exhibited all the school-ready qualities many teachers appreciate. Because Mario was accustomed to being read to and knew the alphabet by sound and recognition of both lowercase and uppercase letters, he often was bored when students gathered on the carpet for letter time. When the teacher would ask students if they wanted to join her on the carpet, Mario would join until the lesson turned to the information he already knew and then quietly go to a different part of the classroom to find a book he wanted to read or a toy he found interesting.

The teacher began to send notes home to Mario's parents letting them know he was struggling to pay attention to lessons and was becoming a distraction to the other 11 students. When Mario's mom asked for more information and learned he was leaving carpet time during the lessons on letters, she explained to the teacher that Mario already knew his letters. She suggested that he might need opportunities to do other things during letter time. Instead of taking the suggestion, the teacher replied with a recitation of school policy and the importance of young children learning the value of being able to sit still during instruction even if the instructional content does not appeal to them in the moment. The teacher said that she and the classroom aide would not have time to develop and provide differentiated lessons or learning opportunities.

On one occasion, the teacher was going over a lesson on letters, and as usual, Mario left the circle; however, this time he was intrigued by a class enjoying some outside time in the school courtyard. He quietly left the classroom without the teacher or the aide even realizing he was gone. Only when the teacher from the other classroom brought him back did the teacher and aide become aware of what had happened. Mario's parents were called in to address the issue, and this is the point at which my support was requested.

Communicating with the teacher and the principal, I learned the teacher did not believe Mario knew his letters because she had not taken the time to assess him. She also believed he was leaving the class because of behavior issues and suggested he be tested for attention deficit hyperactivity disorder (ADHD) to be sure he did not have a learning disability, which she believed was the actual cause of his distractions. The teacher had not explored other ways to engage Mario, and as she explained to his parents, the school had rules for behavior that Mario was having difficulty following. After an intense discussion, the school agreed to test Mario for giftedness and found that he was, indeed, several years above his peers academically.

Kindergarten is ground zero for students learning about the institution of school. Students are expected to learn and follow set rules of engagement. These rules are meant to indoctrinate students into the game of school. When students operate beyond the boundaries being thrust upon them, the institution finds mechanisms to get them in line. The need for Mario's teacher to hold him to a false notion of what it means to exhibit school-sanctioned behavior led her down a dangerous path that, without support for Mario's parents, could have placed him in a situation forcing him into academic services he did not need. This teacher was more concerned with the purpose and rules of the school than she was with her student. She missed an opportunity to enhance Mario's experience because she pigeon-holed his behavior as negative rather than recognizing the need to find out what he knew and differentiating accordingly.

The dimension of race needed to be addressed. Mario was the only African American child in his class. His teacher's unwillingness to recognize his abilities and instead to see him as possibly needing special education services because he did not follow the rules of school behavior confirmed the research about how White teachers tend to see Black students, especially boys, through a deficit lens (Bryan, 2017; Wright & Counsell, 2018). In conversations with Mario's parents, I learned the teacher's biases and disregard were affecting his psyche. His mother described how he would come home from school and tell her he was bad, and although he was usually outgoing and talkative, he was becoming quiet and reserved.

After the school meeting, Mario's parents began taking him to school as a precaution to make sure things were going well. While waiting in line one morning, one of Mario's classmates looked at Mario's dad and said, "Mario's bad, and he's going to jail." His dad asked the child what she meant, and she told him Mario can't sit still and he doesn't know how to follow directions. How did Mario's classmate come up with the idea about him being bad and headed for jail? How did she learn Mario purportedly did not know how to follow directions? Such messages were part of the classroom culture, and students joined in the teacher's sentiments, thereby creating a hostile learning environment for Mario.

This case offers some critical lessons:

- Teachers set the tone for how students experience school.
- Teachers are critical partners in the school socializing process.
- Teachers can create hostile environments for students who do not fit the mold of school-sanctioned behaviors.
- Students pick up their teacher's biases about their peers and can increase a sense of hostility.
- Students of color are particularly vulnerable to a teacher's belief system.
- Students may internalize their teacher's feelings and behaviors toward other students the teacher has shown to be "problematic."

Protecting the Position

Teachers are most likely to work to protect their positional power in four common areas: (1) instructional/pedagogical leadership, (2) language use, (3) grading, and (4) intellectual leadership. Each of these relates to the teachers' professional identities as they understand themselves and their job.

Instructional/Pedagogical Leadership

According to Anderson (1987), among the limited spheres teachers traditionally control, their main locus of control is their classroom. In fact, one of the leading factors for why teachers, especially teachers of color, leave the profession is a *lack* of autonomy related to how they make curricular and instructional decisions (Dixon et al., 2019; Dunn, 2018; García & Weiss, 2019; Griffin, 2018; Lambert, 2006). The classroom remains the place where teachers still have the most control over their lived professional experiences. After all, teachers are the primary persons in charge of what students learn, how students learn, the tools and processes students will use to demonstrate learning, and how their learning will be assessed, at least formatively. Teachers also control students' access to learning by determining which students get to participate in learning and to what degree. Teacher's beliefs and ideologies create a frame that determines which students get access to high-quality assignments and which students they will recommend for advanced courses (Perry et al., 2003).

As described earlier, TNTP's 2018 research study demonstrated clear disparities in student access to high-quality instruction and assignments. The study showed White students received higher access to grade-level and advanced coursework opportunities in 7 out of every 10 classes they observed, and students of color received the same access in only 4 out of every 10 classes observed. Studies conducted by The Education Trust (Patrick et al., 2020) reveal similar differentials in how student populations are more or less likely to be recommended for advanced courses such as honors, AP, and IB. These differentials demonstrate the power of teachers to control the access students have to a high-quality education within their buildings. Although many teachers might include students in aspects of the learning environment such as seating, offering ideas for classroom rules, or limited choice on assignments, they remain the primary decision makers, wielding tremendous power over the trajectory of their students' educational journey.

Pedagogical decisions about how to deliver instruction is the primary area around which most teachers protect their position. We teachers take our ability to do the thing we call "teaching" very seriously, and we bristle at the suggestion that this *thing* over which we have the most control may be up for discussion, review, or evaluation, or may need to be changed in some way.

Think about your last teacher observation. How did you feel going into it? What were you most concerned about? How did you feel during the debrief? If you're like me, the thing I worried most about was having to possibly explain or justify a teaching move. I felt my leaders may not have fully understood my thinking and would want me to adopt strategies that I did not believe would work for *my students*. I leaned heavily into what I thought was best for my students and really did not enjoy hearing that I might not be engaging them in the most effective way. Hearing something about my teaching from someone whom I considered a community outsider was difficult, especially the longer I stayed in the classroom.

As beginning teachers, we tend to eagerly seek feedback; however, once we've been in the classroom for a while and grown accustomed to less frequent observations, we tend to rest on familiar pedagogical structures and may not always reflect on whether those strategies are engaging our students effectively. When someone challenges those structures, we push back—especially if our students show growth or mastery as measured on whatever high-stakes assessment we administered in any given year. After all, if our students are growing and demonstrating mastery, we must be doing something right, correct? We take an "if it ain't broke, don't fix it" mentality, nod our heads at whatever feedback we receive, close our doors, and go right back to our pedagogical comfort zones. Of course, there are times when feedback about pedagogy is legitimate and needs to be taken seriously because children are not being served well. Out of indignation or hurt, we may even double down on our strategies, making our students pay for our wounded feelings.

The protective scenario is especially true if we work in a school where the leader tends to institute initiatives often. I coached in a building where a principal was known for being a serial program initiator. Whenever she attended a workshop, her teachers knew to be on the lookout for a new pedagogical shift. They braced themselves for what they knew would be a requirement to add another tool to the ever-growing repertoire.

In my opinion, we can never have too many ways to help students understand and learn material; however, in this case, the teachers seldom had opportunities to incorporate the new instructional strategy long enough to determine its effectiveness before they were asked to adopt another, and so their protective behavior might be justifiable. In their need to stave off the relentless pedagogical shifting, many teachers played along, incorporated newly required structures when they were being observed, and reverted to their familiar strategies when not being observed.

Let me introduce you to a teacher I'll call Ms. Miles. Ms. Miles taught in a Title I middle school where I coached. Early in our relationship, I was surprised and pleased to have a teacher who was seemingly so eager to have my support. She invited me to observe her teaching, requested that I model the use of suggested instructional strategies and provide ways to increase the rigor of her classroom tasks, and even invited me to model lessons while she took notes and asked all the right questions during our debriefs.

After about three months of observation, I noticed something about Ms. Miles's classroom. Despite having spent considerable time with me, she continued to use disengaging instructional strategies, and the quality of her assignments was unchanged. Her students remained severely below grade level. In discussions with the building leader, I learned I was not the first coach assigned to Ms. Miles or the first to have observed this pattern of behavior. It appeared Ms. Miles had adopted this pattern to demonstrate she was working on the concerns raised during her midyear and annual evaluations.

In getting to know Ms. Miles, I asked her to share her educational philosophy so I could better understand her perspective and instructional choices. I learned she believed she was the person responsible for her students' learning and wanted to be sure they succeeded. I have not met a teacher who did not have a similar philosophy. Unfortunately, she demonstrated her beliefs in protective and disenfranchising ways. She held firm to the "sage on the stage" model of instructional delivery and repeatedly ignored suggestions to incorporate other instructional moves and strategies, even though she pretended to seek coaching support. She had strict guidelines students were expected to follow and did not accept any deviation.

To appease her building leader and appear to be making progress on the elements outlined in her evaluations, Ms. Miles adopted what

I call a "moving the peas around the plate" philosophy. If you've ever watched young children eat peas, you know they get very good at looking like they're eating them by moving them around the plate. They eat a few and spread the rest out. By asking for observations, model lessons, and examples of ways to increase rigor, Ms. Miles could look as though she was taking the feedback to heart and working to improve her instruction without actually making the changes her students needed. She was more wedded to her beliefs about which students could be successful with grade-level material than she was to trying to prepare *all* of her students for advancing to the next grade level and being successful.

Ms. Miles's students tended to perform well on high-stakes assessments, meaning they would show growth. However, they rarely demonstrated mastery or moved to being on grade level. Because she believed growth was most important, she focused on making sure her students demonstrated growth on their tests. She saw no reason to change her repertoire; therefore, she chose to move the peas around her plate. She enacted these protective measures to assume the posture of response only to close the door and revert to familiar ways.

Ms. Miles's behavior is commonplace among teachers, especially those whose students tend to fare well, those who have been in a school building or system for a long time, or those who have grown weary of educational shifts that do not align to their beliefs about their role and maybe about the student populations they may be asked to teach.

From this case we learn the following set of important lessons:

- Teachers' beliefs about students shape how they educate them.
- Teachers choose how and whether or not they will respond to instructional feedback.
- Teacher's choice about whether or not they respond to feedback is a form of exercising instructional power.

Language Use

Earlier in this book, we explored teachers' use of language as a means of protection. Here, let's revisit Amy's classroom, which we first encountered in Chapter 1.

As you'll recall, Amy held a correctionist attitude toward her students' use of language. Grounded in a fixed-language ideology, she required her students to adhere to strict parameters and rules governing speech in her class. Her language system fell within the Dimension IV/Disenfranchising quadrant of instructional power.

During one of my visits to her class, students were completing a writing activity. About a fourth of the class had been out on a field trip, and they returned while their classmates were working on the assignment. Having been a middle school teacher myself, I have come to realize that no matter what a teacher does, middle schoolers are going to talk; it's part of who they are. Unfortunately, Amy didn't allow such typical middle school behavior. As they entered the class, returning students did so in true middle school fashion—laughing, asking questions about the work, and adjusting themselves to their academic environment.

Amy's use of language in expressing her anger at the new arrivals was quite interesting. She responded to their behavior by saying, "I don't know why you came back interrupting my class; we weren't sitting here waiting for you to get back. And just so you know, y'all ain't getting no extra time just because you were on that trip. Your essays are due at the end of class just like everybody else." What's interesting here is Amy's use of the kind of language ("y'all ain't getting no extra time") she worked hard to get her students *not* to use. Her own use of casual register was acceptable; however, her students' use of it was unacceptable.

Additionally, Amy's words communicated her stance on students' position in the room: the class was hers. The phrase "my class" signaled ownership of the physical space and her power lens about her position as the leader. Her statement about the class not waiting for their classmates to return signaled annoyance at students having to be out because of a field trip.

Now, we can argue students should have entered the classroom with better decorum; however, one has to wonder why the adult in the room felt it necessary to make such a statement instead of simply redirecting them or reminding them of how they should enter. In using the same English variety her students used, Amy actually lost credibility regarding her need to engage in correctionist behaviors. Finally, her use of disenfranchising language created an environment where adult language had flexibility not afforded to the students. In this way, Amy's language flexibility led to an exercise of power her students would have been chastised for.

From this case we learn the following:

- Teachers' language is a signal of their power lens.
- Teachers' use of language is an indicator of the relationship between them and their students.
- Expectations regarding how teachers and students use their language must be consistent.
- Teachers' power lens will direct how they view their use of language compared to how they allow their students to use their language.

Grading

Along with pedagogical decisions and language use, grading is another area teachers work very hard to protect. As Joe Feldman (2018) from Crescendo Education Group shows in his work, teachers' grading methods vary widely. This variance creates educational inequities across many lines, including, but not limited to, race, economics, and gender. In my own experience as a classroom teacher, discussions with colleagues about grading were always contentious as we worked to preserve our autonomy. We never wanted anyone to tell us how to grade our students because we felt we knew best what our grades meant. We believed we were the best source of information about our students' academic success. Even with the best intentions, we never all graded the same way unless we were using multiple-choice assessments. When it came to projects, we all had different policies on whether to grade students on behavior, class participation, and homework, or how to account for late assignments. We bristled against any push from our administrators to develop a uniform grading system. The most we would allow was a mandate to ensure we had a sufficient number of grades so students would not be hamstrung by too few.

You read my story in Chapter 5 about how I used a grade to signal to a student, Marian, who was in charge. Understanding the role grades play in students' educational trajectories is a critical element in recognizing how grading becomes a lever for the misuse of power.

During the coronavirus pandemic, when many schools moved to remote learning, some teachers began failing students at very high rates. One teacher I was called in to coach was failing more than 90 percent of his students. Upon investigation, the principal learned the teacher was grading students on class participation and had not even informed students of their impending failures, nor had he informed the parents. Additionally, he afforded students no opportunities to make up missing work or to turn in late work.

Now, I'm all for holding students to high standards and am a firm believer in deadlines; however, such a high failure rate from a single teacher requires serious examination. The grades in this case were not about the teacher helping his students learn from failure. Students did not receive any feedback on their work; there was no evidence of the teacher having conferences with his students to develop an understanding about where they were in the semester and what they could do to improve. This teacher came to the end of a nine-week period, looked at his grade book, and decided that more than 90 percent of his students were going to get an *F* on their report card for that class.

Let me offer another disclaimer about failure. If a student has done nothing in a class—meaning the student has turned in no work, has not demonstrated mastery on assessments (both formative and summative), and there has been a documented, concerted outreach to the student and the parents/caregivers—then the student may have to fail the class. However, this scenario did not apply in this case. This scenario demonstrated a teacher using his power to signal to students that he was in charge of their academic future. Such a situation required the principal to intervene and set up a recovery system to give students an opportunity for redress.

Although failing grades are problematic at any grade, they are especially difficult in high school. Grade point averages have a tremendous impact on students' future and are very hard to overcome. Research by the National Research Council (2011) has shown that students who fail a class are more likely to drop out of high school. Additionally, research by Allensworth and Easton (2005, 2007) found that "ninth graders who were on-track at the end of the freshman year were 3.5 times more likely to graduate than the students who ended their freshman year off-track" (p. 66). Although the study made tacit connections to specific grades, being "on track" is specifically tied to passing grades and courses. When students are failing their classes, they see no path forward and thus leave the system.

Morris (2016) has written about how school systems push Black girls out. Well, grades are part of that process. They can be weapons used against students in ways that can have devastating consequences. As with all other areas in society, students from groups that society has decided do not deserve compassion or patience or opportunity are hit especially hard when teachers use grading as a weapon to wield their power.

From this case we learn some important lessons:

- Grades are a powerful tool for assigning value to students.
- How teachers perceive the role of school will shape how they use grades to protect the institution and their position.
- Grades direct students' access to academic and nonacademic opportunities.

Intellectual Leadership

One of the areas teachers work hardest to protect is related to their position as the intellectual leader in their classroom. The ascribed authority to help students learn "stuff" and learn how to "do stuff" implies tremendous power. The teaching position comes with certain assumptions about the young people in front of you. Many of the assumptions are tied to believing students are blank slates, needing to be filled. Philosopher John Locke introduced the theory of *tabula rasa*, the assertion that the mind is a blank sheet until experience in the form of sensation and reflection provides basic materials, such as ideas, to fill the blank spaces. Although a lot of work has been done to refute Locke's premise, many still hold onto this ideology, especially when it involves students whose families are experiencing economic distress. There's a belief that economic distress affects intellectual or cognitive capacity, and students from families experiencing economic uncertainty are devoid of the knowledge necessary to be successful in school. Nothing could be further from the truth.

You may have heard of the research on the "30-million-word gap" (Hart & Risley, 2003). This research purports to show the effects that living in poverty has on a child's ability to learn, touting the notion that students living in poverty hear 30 million fewer words upon entering school than students not living in poverty. What has not been sufficiently discussed is how the study has been refuted because the initial results were not replicable, and replicability is critical for studies to be considered reliable. This study and others like it are not only used to support biased belief systems; they also create opportunities for students to be treated as though they are deficient, thereby shaping the lens through which a teacher perceives them.

Imagine being a teacher whose beliefs about poverty are grounded in deficit ideologies primarily focused on blaming people as opposed to having a system-level understanding of how people can end up in economic distress. Now imagine having a student in your classroom whose family is in economic distress. You believe the student has special academic needs and is most likely behind the other students in your class, and during a lesson on, say, geology, this student raises a question about the information you present. Given what you believe about students in poverty, the student's pushback is likely to cause you to feel intellectual threat. First of all, you are the adult responsible for the content in the class; second, you probably know more about geology than the student—or at least that is what you believe; and lastly, this student is from a "poor" family and cannot possibly possess enough knowledge on this topic to challenge the information you are presenting. Your reaction might be sarcasm, anger, indignation, maybe even outrage. If you're responding sarcastically, then your language becomes the vehicle through which you are messaging your underlying beliefs to students. This is the protective posture many teachers assume with students who they believe lack certain intellectual abilities due to exigent circumstances. Language becomes the tool that evidences the Protective dimension, which can very easily devolve into the Disenfranchising dimension.

Assuming a protective stance regarding your position as the intellectual leader in your classroom can have devastating effects on students. Not only do teachers assume this posture with students whose families experience poverty, they also do it with students identified as having learning exceptions, those adding English to their language repertoire, and students of color, especially African American students. By now you may be getting weary of my repeated use of the phrase "especially African American students." Believe me, this is no easy assertion to keep repeating; however, the data do not lie.

When studies like *The Opportunity Myth* (TNTP, 2018) show that only 4 in 10 classes with a majority of African American and other students of color get access to grade-level materials compared to 7 in 10 of classes with a majority of White students, and when students make statements like that from a student in Rhode Island who told me, "We have intellectual segregation in this school, and it is clear who gets what," the point must be repeated. I would like nothing more than for this statement not to be true. Unfortunately, it is.

This reality leads me to return to another point about teachers assuming a protective posture regarding intellectual leadership. Students of color are especially vulnerable to teachers who feel threatened in this area. The preexisting power dynamics are already at play, and the additional layer of beliefs about race and ethnicity amplify the situation. If teachers view students through a deficit lens because of a lingering belief in the refuted science about races being intellectually different—even without fully realizing this—those teachers will respond from a Dimension III/Protective or Dimension IV/Disenfranchising space. They will react in ways that disenfranchise the student as they seek to gain back their place as the leader.

In my work in schools across the United States, I have repeatedly seen teachers using bullying tactics as a way to keep their position as the intellectual leader in the classroom. This behavior takes on many forms as teachers move on a scale from overt practices to covert practices. The following is a case in point.

An algebra teacher I worked with, whom I'll call Ms. Washington, taught some classes whose students her school deemed "high flyers" and others considered to be of mixed ability. During my visits, I noticed interesting shifts in the nature of her interactions with students, based on the academic level of their class. These changes went beyond adapting to each class's unique dynamic; her reactions in the mixed-ability class teetered on dislike for the students themselves. She appeared to resent having to teach students she felt were not capable of learning.

During one of my visits, I noticed that in her first class of the day, a class of high flyers, Ms. Washington demonstrated concern for every student. She greeted every child at the door, and the class began with the required "Do Now" activity, but it was centered on building community. Students were asked questions about how they spent their time after school. She wanted to know if they had questions about the homework and gave students time to share their responses with their peers. Linguistically, Ms. Washington exhibited many signs of the Agentive dimension, which I was excited to hear and see in action.

The class was working on a writing exercise about a math problem, using school-issued Chromebooks. Ms. Washington outlined the goals for the day, which were for students to complete a portion of their writing, share with a peer to get feedback, and be prepared to share in their "author's chair" time. Students were seated in pairs with their writing peer, speaking freely about their math problem with their partner as needed. Ms. Washington moved about the classroom, met with students at their request, and only addressed the whole class to remind them of their time and to signal movement to the author's chair segment.

In this class, Ms. Washington cultivated an agentive atmosphere. It's important to note that this school was considered low performing. A majority of its students were on free and/or reduced lunch, about 25 percent were English language learners, and about 60 percent were students of color. Teachers were expected to follow the curriculum with little to no deviation, thus demonstrating Minimal Curricular Autonomy or Restricted Curricular Autonomy. Despite the curricular boundaries, with this class Ms. Washington created a learning environment that demonstrated a belief in students' abilities to understand and complete the assignment with little direct instruction.

Conversely, in the last class of the day, made up of what she might describe as her "worst, lowest-performing students," Ms. Washington exhibited a completely different belief system. She was tired; the kids were tired or ill-behaved (if "talking" is the definition of *ill-behaved*).

And lowest performing? Roughly 20 percent of the students in this class tested one or two grade levels below their current grade. What I noticed, however, was interesting enough to make me think about the excuses related to which students deserve which kind of opportunities to learn and in what kind of environment.

As with her first class, Ms. Washington was at the door to greet her students; however, her greeting was not a hello and a query about their day but a "Come in. The 'Do Now' is on the board. Get to work." Desks had been separated, and the students sat in rows instead of pairs. Ms. Washington explained the goals of the day, which mirrored those in the earlier class, but students were given strict timeframes for the work. They had 15 minutes to complete their math writing drafts in silence. If students spoke during this time, Ms. Washington reminded them it was not the time to talk. Her language signaled that her students needed more boundaries, and her tone was borderline angry. When a student had a question about how to explain his thinking and attempted to ask a classmate, Ms. Washington responded, "It is not the time to talk. If you have a question about your work, you are to ask me. Your classmates won't have the answers."

Once the writing time was over, Ms. Washington paired students, asked them to move their desks together, and handed out sheets of paper with three questions each pair was to ask one another about their writing. They were to write the responses in complete sentences and get her initials to demonstrate completion. Students were only allowed to ask the three questions on the paper. One student requested permission to ask an additional question, and the request was swiftly denied.

For the author's chair segment of the lesson, students had to separate their desks again and close their laptops to a 45-degree angle. When one student did not have her computer at the required angle, Ms. Washington stopped the class and said, "Everyone, turn your computers facing me. Kara [a pseudonym] has decided she does not know how to close her computer to 45 degrees—because I have not said this a thousand times—so you'll have your computers facing me." Needless to say, this exchange was disenfranchising to the students. The language here was a clear signifier of the environment, which can be described as Dimension IV/Disenfranchising.

The students in the first class did not have to close their computers; they were allowed to talk freely among themselves and were not required to complete the peer-question sheet or get initials for proof of completion. Now, before you say, "Well, maybe the last class needed that kind of structure because of their level, or behavior, or some other criteria," consider this: this observation occurred in the second half of the school year, well after the holiday break, when classroom resets normally take place to get students back in the groove of school. By the second half of the school year, it is reasonable to expect students to have the freedom to monitor their behavior as the first class had enjoyed.

In debriefing with Ms. Washington about my observations, she said the first class was easier to manage because the students did not talk as much and she felt she could be herself more. She connected with the first class more because, in her words, "They're able to handle more freedom; I don't have to tell them what to do as much; and they grasp the concepts faster so I can get through more of my material and get through it faster." She went on to explain, "That last class talks too much, and I can't be myself with them. They ask a lot of questions about me, and I just don't want to share with them. Unlike my first class, I just don't feel that connected." Ms. Washington was also concerned about the level of the class and shared the following: "This class is also below grade level, so they need more structure. They can't do the kind of writing I need them to do like my first class. If I didn't give them tight directions, they wouldn't know how to write anything. You should see their writing. That's why I have them write in complete sentences on everything. If I don't, they won't do it. This class just needs more because they're so far behind and so low."

The clear cultural, academic, and relational differences Ms. Washington felt toward her students reveal a stance worth examining. By her own admittance, she felt more connected to the students in the first class and believed they were more capable; therefore, she provided those students a more agentive, engaging, and rigorous learning experience than in the last class of the day. Ms. Washington's beliefs about the students' ability and her comfort level with them gave her a sense of ease that eliminated her need for positional protection. In fact, the situation was the opposite. She created a learning environment where the students were able to freely exchange ideas and ask questions of peers as well as of her, and they seemed comfortable in their relationships with both her and their peers. Ms. Washington was not working to protect her position as the intellectual leader or disciplinarian.

In contrast, the last class had her protecting her belief systems about the need for a strict learning environment with tight protocols. When students attempted to move beyond the boundaries, she swiftly redirected them. Her language use signaled that students needed to be placed back in the box. When they did not follow directions as expected, she reprimanded them, and the entire class paid the price. She protected her protocols using Dimension III/Protective and IV/Disenfranchising language tactics of sarcasm and belittling, holding students to tight structures, and reacting negatively when they went astray. Her language use was the primary vehicle for communicating her beliefs and for controlling student learning and movement. Ms. Washington did not appreciate the personal questions the students in her last class asked about her, and she believed they were incapable of doing their assigned work without strict protocols. She appeared to misread the personal questions as intrusive when they actually may have been the students' way of trying to get to know her. In her misreading, she responded with a set of reductive structures, forcing students to interact with her only in the realm of academics. She worked to protect her personal space in ways that she did not use with her first class. Her beliefs about the students undergirded her decisions about how to structure the class.

From this case, we learn some important lessons:

- Language is a communicator of beliefs.
- Values about academic course levels affect students' educational access.
- Teachers' perceptions of student abilities shape how students are educated.
- Relationships are a key factor in how the power dynamic moves in any classroom.
- Students asking personal questions of a teacher can be a sign of a desire for a strong relationship.

As seen with Ms. Washington, some students are allowed to challenge classroom teaching and learning. These students tend to be in what are called honors or advanced classes. The thinking is that the students in these classes are smart enough and therefore possess the intellectual capacity to ask questions and push back on what they're being asked to do or consume as knowledge. Conversely, there are students who, because they are in the so-called below-grade-level classes, are not afforded the same respect of their intellectual capacity, and any attempt by them to challenge or push back on the content or process is met with swift, often harsh reactions. These are the students teachers are most likely to characterize by saying, "These kids don't know anything" or "These kids don't have any background knowledge, and I have to teach them everything." When students in a devalued class dare to exercise their agency, the reaction to the challenge is likely to be negative.

A fine line separates working to protect your autonomy to make critical educational decisions on behalf of your students and working to protect the power your autonomy offers. As we've discussed throughout this book, as a teacher, you go into your role with institutional authority; you are expected to assume a measure of authority in your classroom. The concept of *in loco parentis* still holds, and you are expected to act in the best interest of your students' academic and nonacademic lives. And despite many districts' use of prescribed curricula that could restrict or minimize your instructional autonomy, you are still expected to be actively involved in the educative process to ensure your students learn the curriculum and perform well on low- and high-stakes assessments.

Your responsibilities also require you to use a variety of pedagogies not included in your prescribed curriculum to engage students in the learning. Additionally, you are expected to perform a host of nonacademic duties, affording you a great deal of latitude, which have as much impact on student engagement, connectivity, and learning as the academics. It is in these discretionary spaces (Ball, 1992, 2018) that you make either power-laden decisions that build agency to empower your students or power-protecting decisions that disenfranchise students.

II PAUSE TO REFLECT

How Do You Protect Institutional and Positional Power, and How Can You Break the Cycle?

We've covered the ways teachers protect power—both institutional and positional. The power cycle has to be broken, and doing so requires reflection and intentional change in practice. You can begin by answering the following questions:

- As a student, how were you part of the school sorting mechanism? What type of classes were assigned to you in middle school? What type of attention did you receive?
- If your middle school did not ascribe labels, what do you remember about how students were grouped in your classes? Think about differential treatment of students

based on perceived level. Which students received the most attention from the teacher?

- If your middle school explicitly labeled classes (e.g., "honors"), how were students placed in those classes?
  - What type of attention did they receive?
  - Which students were afforded the most opportunities to answer questions? Which students were not able to participate as much in class?
- As a high school student, what type of classes did you take? Were you in classes deemed "advanced?"
  - How did you gain access to the classes?
  - What was the demographic makeup of most of your classes?

The next part of this reflection exercise involves creating heat maps. Choose two of your classes—the one with the overall most positive environment and the other with the overall least positive environment—and create a heat map for each one, with the following information:

- Class/course: _____
- Number of students: _____
- Gender breakdown (female, male, nonbinary, transgender female, transgender male): _____

When you are protecting the institution of school, you are working to ensure students adhere to the structures of school, upholding the values of the schooling process: excessive following of rules; not questioning policies or procedures; participating in school-sanctioned and favored clubs, events, and sports. For those students who do not find this appealing, there is a loss of connection to the community. Being a student means being part of a community of learners; however, those who do not fit the mold tend to be outside the community.

In what ways do you contribute to the sorting mechanism of schooling? Consider the following:

- What are your student "buckets" (i.e., categories students are in)? Who is where? How do you decide which student goes into which bucket? Do your decisions reflect assumptions, judgments, actualities?
- How are you communicating to your students they are not on a school conveyor belt?
- Which students are you most likely to recommend for academic opportunities beyond your class/course? What factors are you using to make your recommendations?
- Which students are you least likely to recommend for academic opportunities beyond your class/course? What factors are you using to make the decision *not* to recommend students (e.g., in-school leadership opportunities, extended learning opportunities, high school–community leadership programs)?
- In which classes—and with which students—do you most often force adherence to school rules? Classroom rules?
- In which classes—and with which students—do you least often force adherence to school rules? Classroom rules?
- What instructional power components did you notice being exhibited in each of these classes?

Considering your reflections on yourself as a student and the actions you take as a teacher, answer the following questions:

- Where do you see your past influencing your present?
- How has your school experience shaped the decisions you make as an adult?
- What patterns should you keep?
- What patterns might you need to disrupt? ▸

To say these reflections matter in having you look deeply into your instructional mirror is an understatement. If you find yourself giving the same or similar answers to other questions in the Pause to Reflect sections, I will challenge you to take a step back and think through a different lens. Your students are counting on you.

Looking Ahead

As we have learned, location within a particular dimension does not need to be a permanent situation. In the next chapter, we will explore how to move toward Dimensions I/Empowering and II/Agentive.

7 | MOVING TOWARD AGENCY AND EMPOWERMENT

It is a fundamental democratic right for a child to feel safe in school and to be spared the oppression and repeated, intentional humiliation implied by bullying.

— Dan Olewus

Feeling safe at school includes a multitude of factors. Bullying is one of those factors that, when left unchecked and unaddressed, creates an unsafe environment. Discussions about bullying tend to center on student bullying. One of the unspoken forms of bullying happens as teachers enact their instructional powers in ways that disenfranchise their students. All parents and caregivers send their child to school with hopes and dreams for the future. But those hopes and dreams suffer if they learn their child is a victim of bullying, and bullying by a teacher is an even bigger issue to face.

149

Research has been clear about the devastating effects of peer-to-peer bullying (Rigby, 2001). I remember my own experiences of peer bullying in middle school in New Jersey. My family and I moved to a new town shortly after the death of my father, and the school was part of a community where the children had been together since elementary school. I was new, enrolled in the middle of the year, and disliked on general principle. There were no zero-tolerance policies at the time, and I was certainly not going to tell a teacher about my assailants; that would have caused more problems. So I did what many students do: I put my head down, kept quiet, and looked forward to the end of the school year, hoping it would come as quickly as possible.

Although I had issues with peers, I never experienced what a growing body of research has begun to unearth: bullying by a teacher, one of the core components of Dimension IV/Disenfranchising. The use of power to disenfranchise students can be likened to bullying in that "a teacher . . . uses his/her power to punish, manipulate, or disparage a student beyond what would be a reasonable disciplinary procedure" (Twemlow et al., 2006, p. 10). Using research from McEvoy (2005) and Twemlow and colleagues (2006), Terry and Baer (2012) describe causes of teacher bullying and the reason it persists:

> First, teachers may use bullying techniques as a mechanism for classroom management. Second, teachers who were high-achieving students themselves may become frustrated with and bully students who struggle in school, viewing them as uncooperative and difficult. Third, teachers resort to bullying if they were, or are, the victims of bullying themselves. . . . Finally, because teacher bullying is rarely identified or addressed, these teachers are often allowed to remain in their positions and continue to bully students. (p. 24)

Although these researchers focused their work on teacher bullying specifically, I posit that bullying falls under the category of an overall system of student disenfranchisement, and when used with other forms of power abuse, has devastating effects on student identity, belonging, social and emotional well-being, and academic success.

Building-Level Disenfranchisement

School environment is crucial to student success. Every student should walk into a school where adults know the student by name and make intentional efforts to be welcoming. Throughout the school day, the atmosphere should be positive and encouraging. Unfortunately, various factors often create an environment that lacks these qualities.

Negative Assumptions About Behavior

Imagine being a student walking down the hallway with a friend and coming face-to-face with the principal—a situation that makes you a bit nervous (this is the principal, after all). The principal does not acknowledge you, acknowledges you with a reprimand, or acknowledges you but not your friend. This scenario might seem far-fetched, but it is not; I've witnessed it. Principals stop students all the time in hallways, often assuming that the students are misbehaving. The question becomes, what is it about the environment the leader has created that leads the first encounter with a child to a negative assumption? But setting aside the possibility of negativity, when a leader knows one student but not another, imagine what it feels like to be the one your principal did *not* know. Such leader behavior sends the students very clear messages about who matters and who does not.

This scenario is also true for other adults in schools. When students encounter adults, the meeting should begin positively, to the extent possible. Even if the student is engaging in what would be considered poor decision making and negative behaviors, the adult should not be the one to escalate the situation. Unfortunately, too many adults make assumptions about students in their buildings and do not take the time to understand before they react—often negatively. Consider the following example.

An instructional coach who typically visits a school two or three times per week to work with teachers encounters two African American girls who are talking and laughing as they walk down the hallway. The coach registers their laughter as disruptive and stops the girls immediately. Without taking the time to learn why they were in the hallway, she accuses them of being out of class without permission. It turns out the girls were on their way to lunch after having met with their teacher, and they had a hall pass to prove they were observing the school rules.

Among the many questions to be asked here, the main one for me was, why didn't this adult ask the girls what they were doing instead of making an accusation? This coach was not in the building full-time, and she did not know these girls. Her main points of contact were most likely building leaders—namely, the principal or others and the teachers to whom she was assigned. This form of subtle disenfranchisement is common with adults who may not be fully informed about the operational aspects of the school. The underlying racial dynamic is another dimension of this interaction, as research has shown that Black girls receive harsher reactions and punishment for engaging in activities for which White girls would receive a reprimand or no acknowledgment at all (White, 2017).

Restrictive Controls and Punitive Consequences

Schools with Restricted Curricular Autonomy are likely to have varying levels of disenfranchisement. Given the characteristics of many RCA schools (as described in Chapter 1), they tend to have tight controls over students. These controls take many forms across grade levels as leaders and teachers work to socialize students they believe lack the skills required for a safe and orderly environment. Children are held to what are considered high standards; however, such structures lean toward disenfranchisement as students are disciplined via referrals, demerits, or in-school or out-of-school suspension for even the smallest infractions.

I supported a school as the staff were thinking through how to understand what it meant to design and deliver culturally relevant and responsive educational practices. As is my usual practice, I spent time reviewing school policies—a wonderful source for understanding beliefs and ideologies—to gauge where they might be on this journey. During my review, I came across the following items in the Behavior and Dress Code:

- I understand that my child could receive a consequence such as an Out-of-School Suspension if he or she violates the Code of Conduct.
- I will refrain from all disrespectful behavior, including smacking teeth and rolling eyes.

These were just two of a long list of expectations that if not followed would result in a demerit or detention.

Upon further review, I learned the adults in the school took great care in helping the parents and caregivers understand the meaning of a demerit. The policy stated that demerits were tools of correction to alert students and get them back on track to proper behavior and to ensure that the school remained a safe and orderly environment. Demerits were also meant to help students understand that decisions have consequences. A student receiving six or more demerits in a day would receive detention. According to this policy, students could receive a demerit for the following infractions:

- Having poor posture
- Speaking out of turn
- Leaving their seat without permission
- Being out of uniform (e.g., having a shirt untucked, wearing unapproved jewelry)
- Having electronic items visible

Yes, you read the first item on the list correctly. A child could get a demerit for exhibiting poor posture. The goal was to prepare students for the so-called real world, which, supposedly, emphasizes proper posture. And the concern over being out of uniform seemed similarly egregious. Children get out of uniform all day long; they're children! In this code, the first response to children being children was to give them a consequence, not a simple reminder to tuck in a shirt or remove a piece of jewelry (acceptable jewelry included small earrings but not large hoops).

It's important to acknowledge that school safety is a paramount concern. As a former classroom teacher, I've experienced students running through hallways, pushing, play-fighting, and so on, and I fully understand the need to ensure schools are physically, emotionally, intellectually, and psychologically safe for every child. As a parent, I also want my children to be in safe buildings. The goal for every school is to ensure the safety of children. However, in having such stringent rules accompanied by what appear to be even stricter enforcement tools, students have little to no room to be children. I attended a school with uniforms, and my teachers had to remind me several times a day to tie my shoes, pull up my socks, and rearrange my skirt. I was a mess, but at no time was I made to feel as though the usual haphazardness of daily living would result in a punitive consequence. My teachers seemed to understand that my classmates and I would sometimes inadvertently violate the dress code; and when it was clear a violation was deliberate, there would be a discussion, but not detention or a demerit. In preparing students for the real world, schools and districts have to walk a fine line between keeping students safe and creating a sense of fear through draconian practices.

Language Throughout the Building

We've discussed language use earlier in this book, and here it's important to note that its significance is not relegated to single classrooms. Language use is how educators, leaders, and support staff throughout a building signal the overall environment. There is nothing worse than for a student to have wonderful classroom experiences only to encounter support staff who signal an opposite message. The case below highlights my point.

Schools obviously need to be safe, and communication related to safety is critical. I've been in many schools where teachers' use of language gets students to perform the behaviors leading to a safe physical environment while their language creates a disenfranchising environment of fear.

I visited an elementary school in a district that was dealing with bus-related issues. If you've ever been in a building at the end of the day, you know the only thing students want to do is get on their bus and get home. On the day I visited, students were displaced and had to sit in a hallway and wait until their bus arrived. A teacher I'll call Mr. Burns was assigned to monitor the students. He patrolled the corridor with a bullhorn, warning and threatening students to get them to remain silent. They received a steady barrage of "I don't care that it's the end of the day. I betta' not hear you talkin' to anybody. If I hear you talking, you gonna get detention." There was more to the verbal assault, but I'll spare you. I was so alarmed I went to the principal to let her know how students were being treated. In my discussion with her, I learned that Mr. Burns was a classroom aide who was known to have strong relationships with students throughout the building. His tirade was definitely a surprise to the principal. Being switched to a position with control over students seemed to unleash a different, previously unknown side of this educator. His language was harsh and demonstrated a lack of understanding for how the students may have felt about being forced to sit on the floor after school as they waited for their buses.

This is an example of a disenfranchising environment *outside* the classroom. Mr. Burns's use of language devalued the students by threatening detention and expressing a lack of care for the situation. In addition, his walking up and down the corridor while students were on the floor heightened the power differential.

Classroom-Level Disenfranchisement

As shared throughout this book, teachers wield tremendous power at the classroom level. You've read about the need some teachers have to enact power-protecting tactics to protect the institution and their position. There has inevitably been or will be a time when you disenfranchise your students. Being a teacher does not absolve you from being a human, and when you step into your classroom, you bring your entire self. Therefore, it is critical to look into the mirror and recognize that there have probably been times when you acted in ways that made someone else's child feel unwelcomed, unappreciated, undervalued, or unsupported. It is a hard pill to swallow; however, getting to Dimension I/Empowerment and Dimension II/ Agentive requires a hard look at how you have operated in Dimension III/Protective and Dimension IV/Disenfranchising.

As previously discussed, although curricular autonomy can be a signal of the power dimension a teacher may exercise, it is not a guarantee. A teacher with Unfettered Curricular Autonomy can create disenfranchising spaces as much as a teacher with Restricted Curricular Autonomy. What, then, does it mean to disenfranchise a student? To get to this understanding, let's briefly step outside school.

Disenfranchisement is most often associated with the removal of one's right to vote. The Cambridge Dictionary defines *disenfranchisement* as "not having the right to vote or a similar right or having had that right taken away" and further defines it as "having no power to make people listen to your opinion or to affect the society you live in." Taken together, these definitions offer a framework for understanding what can happen at the classroom level to make students feel as though they have no power to be heard or to affect their environment. Classrooms are microcosms of our world, and the extent to which a teacher engages in overt or passive forms of denying students their ability to be fully engaged in their education is the degree to which students will be disenfranchised.

Disenfranchisement occurs on multiple levels and in various forms, including intellectual and social-emotional. As shown in the Power Principle matrix, there are myriad ways intellectual disenfranchisement can happen. One area relates to who gets the most access to learning. As previously discussed, research shows that teachers hold beliefs and ideologies about who deserves to be educated and to what degree, and these beliefs and ideologies manifest in decisions that affect this access. Examples of such decisions include which students get called on more, which students get opportunities to grapple with rigorous content, which students get wait time as a signal of a teacher's belief in the child's ability to think, and which students get rigorous assignments and tasks. Research also reveals glaring disparities along racial lines in relation to these decisions.

Discipline disparities is another area where Dimension IV rears its ugly head. Imagine two students running around a classroom. One student is White, the other a student of color—Black, Hispanic/Latina/o/x. One student gets a reprimand and is told to stop running; the other is addressed by the teacher in a loud, agitated voice and given a referral. This scenario plays so many times in schools, it is its own crime. Students of color are simply viewed through a deficit lens, which plays out in nearly every aspect of their schooling.

You've heard of the school-to-prison pipeline; it operates on the foundation of adult beliefs about students of color, particularly Black boys, beginning in preschool. These beliefs about who is dangerous in school and needs to be controlled create disenfranchising environments buildingwide and in individual classrooms. Consider results from a Yale study that found African American children make up about 19 percent of all preschool students, yet they represent 47 percent of the preschoolers who get suspended (Gilliam et al., 2016). This same study revealed that boys were three times more likely to be suspended than girls and that teachers were more likely to watch the behaviors of Black boys and count their behaviors as potentially problematic, even when the actions of the child did not warrant such attention. The first question here is, why are preschoolers being suspended in the first place? The next question is, are African American preschoolers engaging in behaviors so radically different from preschoolers of other races and ethnicities that the only response is this disproportionate one?

Another study by Gray (2016) found Latino boys to be at higher risk for excessive disciplinary action than their White counterparts, and the same was true for students with identified special needs or knowledge of economic distress. These studies demonstrate the effects of adult bias on decision making, which adversely affects the academic trajectory of all children, but especially children of color and particularly African American boys. The point here is to understand how school creates separate experiences for students of all races, ethnicities, genders, and other categories; however, there are certain groups for whom school is particularly disenfranchising.

In my work with educators, my eyes have become finely tuned to see what others often miss. I can walk into any classroom and within a relatively short period of time know the prevailing dimension at work. It's not just whether students are seated in rows or whether they're in pods; these configurations do not necessarily align to a specific power dimension. I've walked into classrooms where teachers had students in rows and had as much agency moving toward empowerment as any class where students were seated in pods. The inverse is also true. I've been in classrooms where seating arrangement gave an appearance of agency, but the arrangement was a façade for a toxic setting that subjected students to caustic comments; strict, unevenly applied behavior rules; and an overall demoralizing learning environment. It's easy to get caught up in seating arrangements as a marker for student agency and empowerment. There's a common belief that having students seated in rows signals a rigid and unyielding environment, whereas students arranged in pods signals a collaborative environment. We must get past appearances and do a deep examination of the environment to fully understand how the Power Principle dimensions are moving in and through a classroom.

I worked with a teacher I'll call Mr. Miller, whose principal asked for coaching support. Entering the classroom, I was struck by the orderliness. Students were quietly working, and Mr. Miller was walking around checking to be sure they were on task. I was unsure how to help him because it appeared everything was working as it should. As the class progressed, however, I began to notice subtle changes that explained why the principal had asked for my support. Mr. Miller had the class separated into groups around the classroom. One group was clustered in the back working on computers, another was seated in a row by a window, and another was seated closer to the front. At first I believed the groupings to be learning centers where students would cycle through learning experiences to complete assignments. Unfortunately, this was not the case.

I asked students to explain the seating arrangements. One student seated in the back working at the computer explained she was there because she had not turned in her homework. When Mr. Miller noticed that the student was speaking to me, he said, "She knows why she's there. That's where the no-homework students go." The student confirmed the teacher's statement: when students did not turn in their homework, they had to go to the "no-homework zone." I asked if they were allowed to complete their homework and rejoin the class, and the student said no, they stayed in the zone for the entire period.

As I continued my observation, I noticed the students seated near the window only worked on assignments during the early part of the class. They were not actively involved during the main part of the lesson, when direct instruction was taking place. At the end of the class, I learned from Mr. Miller that the school was trying to reduce referrals, and after sending students out of the room only to have them sent back, his solution was to create a space inside the room where, as he described it, "the bad kids could go and not disrupt the kids who want to learn." His rationale was that he had limited time to get his kids to learn the content needed to pass tests and no time to waste on those who did not want to learn or do their work.

What was interesting about the students was their seeming acceptance of Mr. Miller's rules. The students seated by the window sat quietly while Mr. Miller taught those seated more toward the front of the room. Those students seated in the zone did so without argument or protest.

Mr. Miller had created a limiting, stratified learning environment. He exhibited an unwillingness to learn about his students and chose only to educate those he believed exhibited the qualities he valued most. In my discussion with him, it was clear we would need to address some of the underlying beliefs and ideologies leading him to create this isolating learning environment.

This case illustrates the negative effects of a disenfranchising environment. Students were subjected to a stratified, isolating environment that devalued and discounted who they were as people and relegated them to margins of education simply because their teacher took no time to learn anything about them. Here are a few major takeaways from this case:

- Beliefs and ideologies drive instructional decisions.
- Compliance is not a guarantee of learning.
- Creating disciplinary systems that isolate students is disenfranchising.
- It is important to take time to learn about students to better understand them.

Student Perspectives on Teacher Power

In interviewing students across the country to learn about their high school experience, one of my goals was to understand how they processed the concept of teacher power. If you want to know the truth about school, ask a student. These high schoolers represented every class level, race, gender, and ethnicity, and I learned from them.

When asked if teachers used power in their classrooms, the students' overwhelming response was a resounding yes. These students had no qualms in talking about how their teachers used tactics to keep them compliant, sought to manage their speech in and out of the classroom, and used assignments and grades as a tool for exerting power and authority. One student told me, "We have academic segregation in this school. I'm in the advanced classes and I *know* I'm getting a better education than my classmates in other 'lower' classes. This is a terrible feeling, because I don't know how to help them." Another student from a different school shared, "We're corrected every time we talk. We're told we can't talk like this or like that. It's like who we are doesn't matter. It's like they're trying to erase us."

One group of students I interviewed was made to feel the best thing they could do was graduate from high school and leave their community. They were fed a steady diet about the plight of their community and how important it was for them to do well in school so they could leave and pursue better opportunities elsewhere. Imagine that! In this case, possibly well-intentioned adults were sending a message about not just students as individuals but about their entire community. Talk about disenfranchising! And another student told me, "I know I'm not necessarily wanted here. Every time my friends and I walk down the hall, the officers are following us and asking where we're going, but they don't ask the 'other' kids where they're going." This student happened to be African American, and he worked hard not to name who the "other" students were.

These student comments make it easy to see how school environments can be disenfranchising. Adults' use of language evidenced a Dimension IV/Disenfranchising educational environment. But if you were to ask the adults who saw school as a way out about their motivation, they would probably say they believed they were acting in the students' best interests by making that characterization instead of helping students better understand how a neighborhood may have become economically distressed or how their education could be a catalyst for change. Ask the officers in the second example about their purpose and they'd likely tell you it's about school safety; they'd be less likely to recognize how their queries sent a message that certain students create a sense of a lack of safety, whereas "other" students do not.

How Might You Be Disenfranchising Students?

Think of this reflection time as fine-tuning. You're working to fine-tune your eyes and ears to possible blind spots, areas where you might have been disenfranchising your students. As you have learned, much of what we do as teachers stems from our own experiences as students and is tied to our ideologies about people in general, about specific groups of people, and about how we understand the profession of education. It is important to bring forward memories that shape your approach to teaching. These reflections can help to ensure that every student has the opportunity to be empowered in learning.

Student memories
Think of a time when you were the victim of or a witness to a teacher or other adult disenfranchising a child.
- Describe the situation:
  - Grade
  - Class
  - Circumstances/event
  - Did the event happen in front of other students, or was this done privately?
  - How did the adult disenfranchise you or the other student?
    - Yelling
    - Unnecessary sarcasm
    - Belittling
    - Isolation tactics
    - Grading
    - Use of referral/discipline system for minor offenses

- What do you remember about the feeling you had from this experience (as either the victim or the witness)?
- How did you handle this event?
  - If you were the victim, what did you do? How did you handle your feelings (e.g., tell your parents/caregivers, share with a classmate, tell another adult, shut down from learning)?
  - If you were a witness, how did the event affect your relationship with the student? What did you notice about the student's behavior after the event? How did you handle your feelings (e.g., tell other classmates, tell your parents/caregivers, talk with the victim)?
- What did you learn from that experience?

Teacher tactics

Now put your teacher hat back on. Answer the following questions to dig into your own practice. These questions are meant to get at how you use language in your classroom. Resist the urge to view yourself through rose-colored glasses. Take the risk and plunge in.

Think of a time when you have used sarcasm or raised your voice in your classroom.

- Did you use the sarcasm *with* your students or *on* your students?
  - If *on* your students, who was the student/s?
  - What prompted you to use sarcasm or raise your voice?
- How often do you use sarcasm? Raise your voice?
- How do your students react?
  - If a student exercises self-protection (e.g., talking back, using sarcasm on you, possibly resorting to profanity), what do you do?
  - If a student yells back at you, how do you respond?
- What do you learn about yourself from the use of sarcasm or voice raising?
  - Are you using sarcasm and voice raising to protect your position as the one in charge or the smartest person in the room?

Think of a student with whom you have a particularly challenging relationship.

- Who is the student?
  - ○ Gender
  - ○ Race/ethnicity
  - ○ Personality
  - ○ Background details
- What makes the relationship so challenging?
- What role do you play in the challenge?
- Is this challenge indicative of the types of challenges you have with other students like this? (This question is a tough one, but it requires real honesty to see if there's a pattern.)
- Does this student have more positive relationships with other adults?
  - ○ With whom does this student have better relationships?
  - ○ What discussions have you had with other teachers/ adults to learn how to engage more productively with this student?

Overall reflection
- Based on your responses, how might your experiences as a student be influencing your actions as a teacher?
- What learner beliefs from your childhood might you be displaying in your use of disenfranchising behaviors?
- What pattern do you see in your thinking across your classes and the students you teach?
  - ○ Who are the students you are most likely to disenfranchise?
  - ○ In which class are you most likely to engage in disenfranchising behaviors?
  - ○ How are the students in classes where you engage in disenfranchising behaviors performing on indicators of success?
- How is your use of disenfranchising behaviors affecting students' ability to be their full selves in your classroom?
- How is your use of disenfranchising behaviors affecting students' ability to achieve at high levels in your class? ▶

Moving Past Disenfranchisement

Moving past disenfranchisement requires a willingness to think differently about your role as the instructional leader of your classroom. Your role does not diminish if you provide students with the skills they need to be successful at school and in life. In fact, the importance of your role increases because you are helping students to become people who display the types of skills the world needs—people who think critically, advocate appropriately, and are independent.

So, how do you do it? How do you go from disenfranchising instructional power to agentive or even empowering instructional power? It's easy to suggest you look at the characteristics of Dimension I/ Empowering and Dimension II/Agentive and simply do those things. However, you have to deal with your beliefs before you can shift in ways that result in progress. First, you must realize that something in your teaching must change. Next, it's important to *want* a different kind of environment. The change you believe is necessary starts with a clear decision to make structural changes to your practice.

One way to move forward is to be sure you have taken the time to really invest in the reflections throughout this book. Moving away from Dimension IV/Disenfranchising does not mean first shifting to Dimension III/Protective. Remember, the dimensions are not linear; it's important to not take an attitude of "I'll move to Dimension III, and that will be progress." Doing so will not be progress because your students will still be learning in an unhealthy environment. The goal is to support students toward empowerment. Therefore, you must move as quickly as possible to adopt agentive practices on your way to empowerment.

I wish there were a clear road map to empowerment that ensured success if you perform a "Top 10" list of practices. But the dynamic nature of the profession of education guarantees that you will progress and regress along the way. The key is to move forward *because your students deserve it*.

Let's spend some time rethinking practice. The chart in Figure 7.1 offers possibilities for progress. The fourth column provides space

FIGURE 7.1

Moving from *Protective* and *Disenfranchising* to *Agentive* and *Empowering* in Classroom Environment, Language, Learning, and Grading

Protective and Disenfranchising Behaviors	Action Steps to Build Agency	Action Steps to Build Empowerment	Reflection
Environment: Think of your classroom environment as your starting line for success.			
• You have a "hidden curriculum." That is, students are held to standards they have not been made aware of. • You have rigid rules regarding classroom space and how students may move around in your classroom.	• Be fully transparent about your expectations in all areas of learning and behavior. • Collaborate with colleagues on your team, in your department, and in your building to determine the ways elements of a hidden curriculum exist in areas such as dress, speech, decorum, and so on.	• Ask students at the beginning of the year for ideas on classroom layout. • Discuss with your students how best to operate in the physical space. • Pay attention to students who voice the need for individual space. • Consider raising the possibility of providing open spaces throughout your	• What did you try? • What worked?

- Build student understanding about the nature of a hidden curriculum in your building (after you have assured yourself you are not employing one in your classroom).

- Collaborate with colleagues to make all expectations explicit for students.

- Engage students in discussions about classroom layout and how the space can be modified to create an environment they would like. (Note: If you have multiple classes or are teaching young children, you'll need to compromise to accommodate multiple ideas and needs.)

- building, where students can work outside the classroom. Involve students in this discussion about the appropriate ways to engage in learning when outside the building.

- Be willing to discuss the best ways to redirect students for maximum accountability with students.

- What did not work as well as you had hoped?

- What is worth trying again?

(continued)

FIGURE 7.1 *(continued)*

Moving from *Protective* and *Disenfranchising* to *Agentive* and *Empowering* in Classroom Environment, Language, Learning, and Grading

Protective and Disenfranchising Behaviors	Action Steps to Build Agency	Action Steps to Build Empowerment	Reflection
Language: How you use your words and how you expect and allow students to use their words are critical aspects of your exercise of instructional power.			
• Your language is caustic and often sarcastic. You resort to yelling and using power-laden, "ownership" phrases to suggest students are visitors in your space instead of partners in learning. • You use suggestive language to get students to do what you want them to do.	• Check your tone. Consider taping a lesson or series of lessons. How do you sound? • Use collective language instead of possessive language (*we* vs. *I*, when it authentically applies; *our* vs. *my*, etc.) • Avoid a correctionist approach.	• Use student colloquialisms as a way to connect them to content. • Allow students to choose the language variety that best fits how they understand content and that fits the audience and tasks. • Be sure that English language learners are able to freely use their home language as a bridge builder to content.	• What language adjustments did you make? • What language decisions do you notice your students making? • How are students' language decisions affecting the classroom environment?

- Be clear with students about how you want them to use their language.
- Seek to understand students' colloquialisms.
- Use direct, specific language to eliminate any confusion as to whether students have choice in a particular matter or situation. If you want students to do something, ask them directly, keeping in mind that "please" and "thank you" go a long way.

- Build student knowledge about the difference between suggestive and direct language to help them navigate different environments.

- How are students' language decisions affecting their learning?

- How are your language decisions affecting the environment?

- How are your language decisions affecting student learning?

(continued)

FIGURE 7.1 *(continued)*

Moving from *Protective* and *Disenfranchising* to *Agentive* and *Empowering* in Classroom Environment, Language, Learning, and Grading

Protective and Disenfranchising Behaviors	Action Steps to Build Agency	Action Steps to Build Empowerment	Reflection
Learning: Students come to school to learn "stuff" and how to "do stuff." They come to their learning with different levels of readiness, willingness, and interest. Remember, students are asked to get and be excited about content they had no hand in choosing.			
• You repeatedly use prior years' assignments, with no changes. • You are the sole source of information/knowledge.	• Consider students' needs and adjust as necessary. Do not focus on scaffolds but on content at the grade level. • When a student demonstrates productive struggle, use an inquiry model to understand where the student needs help; do not assume you know. Ask the following questions: "Where are you stuck? When did you get stuck? Is this about knowledge or skill?"	• At the beginning of the year (if possible), review your learning standards with your students; enlist them in developing a list of topics they want to learn about to meet those standards. • Enlist your students in project design, shaping a learning unit from content to assessment to activities. • When students demonstrate productive struggle, have them engage in the inquiry	• What did you try? • What worked?

- What did not work as well as you had hoped?

- What is worth trying again?

model described in Column 2 with chosen classmates.

- Redesign your learning tasks to foster student independence and authentic peer collaboration. Involve students at the outset to gauge where they are in their learning and skill development. Involve them in the design of learning, grouping, grading scales, materials selection (where available). Rearrange seating (if possible) to ensure students can collaborate effectively and have open access to materials (digital and print).

- Consider giving students a task that requires collaboration—beyond sitting together and sharing answers. Be sure students have access to all materials, and give them a designated time to complete the task. Be available as a resource.

Note: These questions require a conversation with your students about the difference between what they know and what they can do.

- Review your learning plans to determine who is doing the majority of the work. Determine how much time students will be engaged in knowledge and skill building versus how much time you are engaged in delivering instruction.

- Review your learning plans for opportunities to engage students in building knowledge; restructure student learning to build both collaboration and independence.

(continued)

FIGURE 7.1 *(continued)*

Moving from *Protective* and *Disenfranchising* to *Agentive* and *Empowering* in Classroom Environment, Language, Learning, and Grading

Protective and Disenfranchising Behaviors	Action Steps to Build Agency	Action Steps to Build Empowerment	Reflection
Grading: Grading sends a message of value. It is among the most power-laden forces a teacher can have. How you assign value to students' work is a critical lens into your belief systems, biases, and power ideology.			
• You grade students on participation (e.g., hand raising, classroom behavior, bringing in classroom items). • You grade students on effort.	• Analyze which students participate in the ways you most value. Review these students' grades compared to other students. What do you notice? • Involve students in a discussion about participation. Share your values on participation, learn theirs, and collaborate with them on how best to account for participation.	• Enlist students in creating grading structures (learn what matters to them). • Offer a variety of grading structures. Remember there is no right or wrong way to assess students. The type of knowledge should dictate the type of assessment, which dictates the type of instruction and activities students need to demonstrate both mastery and opportunities for advanced knowledge building.	• What did you try? • What worked?

- Build students' knowledge about various types of assessment and grading. At the start of each unit, explain the type of knowledge they will build, the skills they are expected to develop, and how they will be assessed and graded. Build their understanding on the assessment and grading format (even if they are engaged in standardized assessment).

- At various times of the year (preferably at the beginning), explain to students your stance on effort (i.e., what does it look like, why it matters, how you determine it).

- Invite students to share their ideologies about effort (i.e., what it looks like to them, how they determine it).

- Come to a consensus on how or if effort will be factored in as part of their grade.

- Where applicable, invite students to determine the connection between the knowledge they are building and the type of assessment and grading methods necessary to best demonstrate mastery.

- Remove effort from your grading criteria. Instead, have students include statements about their depth of preparation, engagement, and completion.

- What did not work as well as you had hoped?

- What is worth trying again?

for your reflections about the impact of your "experimentation." This chart is not meant to be an exhaustive list of possible action steps; rather, it is a starting point. As you try these, seek support from your colleagues (you may find wonderful examples of agency building and empowerment in your building) and build your own bank of actions to support your students.

The areas covered in Figure 7.1 are just a few of those where you can move from protective or disenfranchising to fostering authentic agency and empowerment. The ultimate goal is to develop empowered students.

Looking Ahead

Empowerment can seem scary because it is about individuals making decisions in their own best interest, not in their best interest as we define it. As you begin to shift toward empowerment, you will have to be prepared for the changes in you and in your students. This shift can be bumpy, as you consciously decide to step back from the traditional teacher role into a place where you exhibit enough trust in your students to remove the barriers created by your unknown or unresolved ideologies and educational philosophies.

In Chapter 8, we will explore what it means to be ready for agentive, empowered students. We will also discuss how to help your students navigate the terrain of empowerment—especially if the only place they get to exercise it is in *your* classroom.

8 | ARE YOU READY FOR AGENTIVE AND EMPOWERED STUDENTS?

You can. You should. And if you're brave enough to start, you will.

— *Stephen King*

The quote from Stephen King frames this last chapter of the book. Moving students to empowerment by building their agency might seem like a daunting task, but rest assured—you *can* do this and you *should* do this. That said, it will require you to be brave enough to start making critical changes to how you think about your role as an educator and what you believe about what your students can do.

Moving Toward Empowerment

We've been on quite a journey over these last chapters. Although possibly exhausting, the task of digging into your ideologies, educational experiences, and educational philosophy was meant to be liberating. Those 1,500 decisions you make on a daily basis may have uncertain origins. If you're like me, you've found yourself making a comment or decision only to stop and wonder, "Where did that come from?" The goal of this book has been to help you have answers to that question so you will be able to make the type of decisions that will benefit your students while ridding yourself as much as possible of those ideologies that lead to harmful, regrettable decisions.

In this chapter, we will learn about students who get opportunities for agency and empowerment, preparing yourself and your students for agency and empowerment, and guardrails that students might need as they begin to exercise agency and move toward empowerment. As in the other chapters, you will do some unpacking of your practice, be asked to try something different, and consider the outcomes. After working through the exercises in this chapter and reflecting on the ones from previous chapters, you should be well on your way to fostering or deepening your students' agency and moving them toward empowerment.

Who Gets to Develop Agency and Be Empowered?

Much of student agency is about adults providing carefully constructed learning opportunities that mimic agency and offer what I call "managed choice"—choice based mainly on goals students themselves may not have chosen or had a hand in developing. It often takes the form of giving students a list of options from which to choose. In many, if not most, learning environments, teachers provide the scope and scale around which students get to make independent decisions, and this is what constitutes agency (Parker et al., 2017).

Consider the times when your students made learning decisions. Were those decisions generated by the students themselves—meaning they chose, independent of content you provided, what they would learn, how they would express that learning, and how they would be assessed on that learning? Consider also your reaction to students who did not operate within the confines of the options you may have provided. How did you feel and react? Were you annoyed by students who recognized they did not actually have the academic freedom they wanted and expressed their frustration by questioning assignments, ridiculing the books chosen, or flat-out refusing to engage in the game of school?

Developing educational agency is a means of providing students with the ability to combine a strong sense of self with a strong sense of their skills to make sound decisions (Freire, 1974, 1985). As Giroux (1984) and Kundu (2020) state, agency is contextual and can be manifested in myriad ways that are grounded in the intersection of social, cultural, economic, political, and educational experiences of the child. Agency should result in opportunities for students to operate beyond the boundaries set by adults; however, this is rarely the case in most schools across the United States.

If school-based agency is contrived, then empowerment is even more so. Because empowerment is about individuals acting on their agency to make self-directed decisions in their own best interests (Drydyk, 2013), it makes sense that students seldom, if ever, get opportunities to move in this direction. Despite educators using the language of empowerment, students simply do not get opportunities to fully actualize empowered decision making. It takes an evolved educator to get students to a place where they exercise their agency to such a degree that empowerment becomes the next level. I must admit, in my work around empowerment and agency, I often wondered how to disentangle the two because I understood building agency was the goal. What I recognize now is the need to build students' skills of agency so they can exercise it through empowerment. As we learned in the first part of this book, agency and empowerment are like first cousins: students need both to become their complete selves. As educators, we know we are likely *not* to witness our students becoming their full selves, but we can develop their agency and empower them to apply it to reach their potential and advocate for themselves.

Empowerment, Agency, and Disparate Discipline

Student empowerment is rare, and although many students have measured, managed agency, such agency is unevenly meted out. Teachers who interpret a student's empowered agentive behavior as defiance, insubordination, or disrespect are likely to respond by expressing their own authority to regain the balance of power (Reeves, 2021). Such reactions often take the form of discretionary discipline reactions such as office referrals, removal from class, as well as in- and out-of-school suspension (Liiv, 2015; Skiba & Losen, 2016). When asked her thoughts about which students are afforded the right to make empowered, agentive decisions, English teacher Erin replied, "I think the students who are most compliant." She went on to share:

> The students who tend to be more agentive get labeled as disruptive, challenging; as [a] problem student, struggling student—whatever these other euphemisms schools use as proxies for "I really can't control this student." Like, those are the students who are rarely ever afforded the right to advocate for themselves in a way that they don't experience negative consequences—i.e., in-school suspension, out-of-school suspension, demerits, exclusion from school activities.

Erin's perspective on who gets opportunities and who does not is supported by research data on discipline showing that a primary reason for disciplinary referrals is perceived defiance—that is, students rejecting structures they believe are not in their best interest or rejecting ongoing poor treatment. Unfortunately, students lack the skills to advocate for themselves, and their frustration leads them to react poorly.

Because schooling mirrors society, we have to acknowledge that not all students are empowered to exercise their agency equally.

There are students whose independent acts of empowerment are perceived as threats in ways that other students' acts are not. National discipline data evidence the disparities in teacher response to students by race, ethnicity, and gender (CRDC, 2014; Liiv, 2015; Reeves, 2021; Skiba & Losen, 2016; Skiba & Peterson, 2000). The data reveal that students of color, especially Black boys, are three times more likely to be disciplined for behaviors such as disrespect, defiance, and dress code violations than their White counterparts. Data also reveal that Black girls are three and a half times more likely to be disciplined for similar perceptions of misbehavior; seven times more likely to have one or more out-of-school suspensions than their White counterparts (CRDC, 2014; Inniss-Thompson, 2017); and nearly five times more likely to be disciplined for policies related to their hair, their voices, and their body than their White female counterparts (Morris, 2016). In fact, studies have shown White girls are the least likely students to be disciplined at school despite committing the same acts of perceived policy violations as other students (CRDC, 2014; Martin & Smith, 2017; Meek, 2009). Given the racial and gender differences between teachers and students, these discipline disparities support a statement attributed to Rabbi Shmuel ben Nachmani: "We don't see things as they are. We see them as we are."

Is it any surprise, then, that although most teachers say they are not biased and believe every child can learn, research by Starck and his colleagues (2020) demonstrates that teachers are just as biased against Black students as the rest of society is against Black people. I'm reminded of a situation my son faced in his 5th grade math class. I was called by his teacher, who was concerned that he was being defiant. When I asked her to explain her position, she shared the following information: "The class took a test today, and your son finished in eight minutes. I asked him twice if he wanted to go check his answers, and he told me no. Finally, I said, 'Look at Marc. He's checking his answers. Don't you want to check yours?" And he said, 'No. I already checked them before I turned in my test.'" I had to be sure

I fully understood her issue and asked this clarifying question: "Did you tell him to go check his work or did you ask him?" She replied, "I asked him." Because my children grew up in a household where when I wanted them to do something, I told them to do it, my son was very clear on the linguistic difference between being asked if he wanted to do something and being told to do something. Being asked signaled a *choice*, which in this instance he did not have, even though his teacher presented her language as such. In this instance, my son was perceived as defiant because he exercised his agency enough to know whether he wanted to check his work or not. His teacher used suggestive language hinting at choice, when what she wanted was for him to go back to his desk and check his work.

The teacher had decided my son needed to be disciplined for not doing what she suggested, showing a complete lack of understanding about her use of suggestive language. That lack of understanding created the opportunity for my son to demonstrate *his* understanding of the words she actually used. Because he did not do what she wanted—remember, she *asked* rather than *told* him—she took his actions to be defiant.

This scenario happens all the time. Teachers play with language in an effort to not appear direct, when in fact their suggestive language is a tool that trips many students up by giving them the false sense that they have choice. That is, when teachers (especially White teachers) use suggestive language, it confuses many Black students whose parents and caregivers tend to use more direct communication. Suggestive language obfuscates a teacher's meaning because if students understand the difference between suggestion and direction, they will exercise their agency and decide whether or not they want to follow a suggestion. If the teacher's suggestion was intended to be a direction and a student chooses to do what my son did, that student is likely to be deemed defiant. This is especially true if there is, as Liiv (2015) and Reeves (2021) suggest, racial differences between the student and teacher, with African American children being more likely to be deemed defiant, insubordinate, or disrespectful than their peers. This personal example illustrates just one of the many ways students find themselves at the mercy of educators who make determinations about who should and should not be able to exercise empowered agentive decision making.

From this case we learn the following:

- Teachers use language to manipulate student behavior and then react negatively when students act on their own behalf.
- Teachers should communicate directly about what they want students to do instead of suggesting, when what they want is compliance.
- Students know the difference between suggestions and directions.

Preparing Students for Empowerment

Have you ever watched a toddler put on a parent's shoes and try to walk around in them? It's a sight to see as the child tries to navigate walking in shoes that are too big. The child wobbles around, the shoes fall off, the child falls and ultimately does not get too far. If students operate as empowered beings enough to exercise agency when they have not been supported to do so, they'll be like that toddler in adult shoes, wobbling around and falling down. They might even run into adverse responses to their empowered agency as adults may misinterpret their actions and exercise their authority against them in punitive ways. Students need guidance; they need to know what agency and empowerment are before they get launched into the deep. Educators need to explicitly prepare them through careful structures that foster understanding, responsibility, and critical decision making (Freire, 1974, 1985; Horton & Freire, 1990).

In moving toward agency, students need knowledge about what it is, how to exercise it, when to exercise it, and how to be prepared for adult reactions to their empowered agentive behavior. To move in this direction, teachers need to give students a solid structure upon which they can build their agency. The example below provides a window into how one teacher began her and her students' journey into educational empowerment and agency building.

You've read about Erin in previous chapters. I interviewed Erin about her power ideology and learned the following. Like many teachers, she did not feel she had instructional power. She stated, "I don't feel as though I have some power [students] don't." As we continued to explore the idea of her being a power-possessing educator, Erin began to extend her understanding and attach it to the decisions she made. Realizing she had Calibrated Curricular Autonomy, she began to reflect on the different cultures of her classes to determine when and how she exercised both her curricular autonomy and how she used her authority to govern student behavior. What she began to understand was that the culture of her classes often dictated the varying levels of power she exerted to foster student learning and engagement.

As teachers, we know full well how different each of our classes can be. One class may afford us the ability to be flexible with our management style and another will require us to be more stringent. Such was the case with Erin. She had two very different classes, which allowed her to examine how to get on the road to building her students' academic agency while adhering to their need for support. Erin's process sheds light on the need to be strategic and careful when embarking on how best to support students in moving toward academic agency and empowerment.

Erin taught two sections of pre-AP English, and she began her agency building with the students in her first-period class. She described these students as possessing a maturity that allowed her to "move to the side of instruction rather than remaining in the front." She realized the maturity of this class one day when she arrived late due to an early-morning building meeting that ran over the scheduled time. When she arrived at the classroom, she found her students had completed the attendance, checked in all the homework, and were discussing the previous night's homework. Her students were aware of the procedures; therefore, they were able to take care of classroom logistics in her absence.

Experiencing her students acting on their agency without her even broaching the topic gave Erin the information she needed in order to examine how she was approaching her instruction with that class. She realized that her students had skills she hadn't previously considered and that she could turn over the class logistics completely to them and focus on designing learning experiences to challenge their intellect. Erin had held fast to the belief that her job included handling the logistics; however, in watching her students, she began to think of them more as educational partners. She shared that this is where the major shift in her teaching began.

Other moments kept Erin on this journey. One lesson was particularly significant in her recollection of how she began to build her students' agency and guide them toward becoming empowered learners. She was leading students through a particularly challenging piece of literature, *Oedipus Rex* (a scenario we explored in Chapter 3). As the lesson progressed and Erin went through the standards-aligned questions; exercises about the play; and the five stages of grief, including a thinking protocol in which students had to collaboratively generate, sort, connect, and elaborate questions and ideas across their poem, one of her students, whom I will call JD, chose not to engage in this exercise. Instead, he chose to write in his journal during class and asked permission to take chart paper home to complete the assignment. Upon returning to class, JD demonstrated a complex understanding of the play and had constructed his own knowledge by deconstructing the text on his own. Because JD worked independently, he had to figure out how best to collaborate with his classmates to expand his understanding and complete the assignment. He had formulated his own set of questions, and he went to each of the groups, asked his questions, engaged in an academic conversation with them, and then returned to his desk to expand his knowledge and complete the final writing assignment.

Erin could have refused his request. She could have viewed his request as an act of defiance and punished him for not doing the work the way she had planned. Instead, Erin chose to relinquish her instructional power; she gave JD his own power to know himself as someone who needed more space than the classroom offered. JD was more in tune to who he was as a learner, and he taught Erin how to help him learn. Because Erin was willing to step aside and learn from JD, she showed him the importance of following his learning instincts. Erin stepped into the Empowering and Agentive instructional power dimensions to support JD in his learning. JD was courageous in requesting the opportunity to take materials home, demonstrating a form of empowerment and agency.

As Erin described her trepidation about giving JD the materials, she admitted to not being sure he would do the work. She also shared that she was more concerned about *not* showing JD trust; that's what led her to step away from her power. Erin said JD taught her the importance of trusting students to know their own instructional and learning needs. JD became the catalyst for Erin's complete revamping of her use of instructional power, leading her to demonstrate elements of the Empowering and Agentive dimensions. Although she always believed students should have a say in their education, Erin said her belief came alive when JD pushed her to give them that say.

Lest you think her decision was easy, remember this. Erin was a second-year teacher in an environment with Calibrated Curricular Autonomy. She had a pacing guide and was expected to adhere to the instructional mandates of her district and building. Hers was not an easy decision. It was a brave and courageous decision.

From Erin's experience we learn the following:

• Students will often be our guide into moving toward Agentive and Empowering instructional power.

- Making the decision to begin building agency and empowerment requires watching and listening to students to see skills we may have missed.
- Taking a first step toward agency and empowerment might seem scary because the outcomes will feel uncertain.

Let's look at what it means to watch students as a means to moving them to agency and empowerment. One of the best places to begin this work is through your existing tasks. Consider your last collaborative task. How did you design it? Were students collaborating (meaning the assignment could only be completed through collective work), or were they completing the task independently?

I've had the privilege of helping educators build lessons, and one area where I've found teachers need the most support is deciding how to develop students as academic leaders. Educators develop assignments and tasks in which students have to assume roles, but they tend to assign roles based on what they believe to be students' academic levels. Although this seems to make sense, teachers' belief systems will intersect with their power ideology, leading them to repeatedly assign certain students to leadership roles. Doing so will create inequitable access to leadership development for students who do not fit the teacher's framework for what a leader looks, sounds, and acts like.

Watching and listening requires a willingness to dispel our usual practices based on judgments associated with outward characteristics to hear the language students use to demonstrate content and leadership skills. One way we can broaden our perspective on student leadership is to hear with a different set of ears. Remember, we hear culture before we encounter it. How we hear students speak shapes what we believe about them. Getting past this tendency requires that we ask ourselves these important questions:

- Is the language my students are using required to demonstrate content-specific mastery?

- Am I bothered because I believe my students are violating my preference for a form of language?

Here's an example to consider. I worked with a high school teacher whom I will call Marie. Her school was more than 80 percent Black, located in the rural South. I asked Marie to explain her thoughts on how students should use language in her classroom. Her response was quite telling. She said, "My philosophy is that as long as students are not having to show they know the content by using English-type words, I say, let your freak vibe fly. . . . Of course, I don't mean they can cuss in class. But I want them to be comfortable speaking." She also shared that her students thought her use of language was too formal, and they challenged her to use their colloquialisms. Remember Beth, introduced in Chapter 2, who was an outsider in her school community? Marie was also an outsider, but she addressed the linguistic differences in a way that acknowledged the cultural-linguistic differences between her and her students. Marie explained that she shared with her students how much she learned from them by how they spoke, and she wanted them to learn about her from how she spoke. In this way, Marie created a leveled power dynamic in an English classroom, where how students use words is traditionally controlled more closely. Letting her students' "freak vibe fly" offered them space to be expressive; it honored their culture but also gave Marie space to be her cultural linguistic self without trying on language that was not her own.

Rethinking Classroom Management

This is the story of a teacher I will call Michelle. To understand her journey, we must begin with the learning context through the lenses of curriculum autonomy. In conversations about her school, Michelle described it as an environment that heavily controlled students. It was a place where students were expected to adhere to strict rules governing their behavior in and out of the classroom, and stepping out of line could mean demerits for things such as not raising their hands before speaking, being out of uniform, or being in the hall without a hall pass. In addition to the strict behavior rules, the curricular autonomy can best be described as Restrictive Curricular Autonomy. The school was considered low performing, and to perform better on high-stakes assessments, administrators expected teachers to be on the same page at the same time. They wanted to walk into one room and hear the lesson begin and walk into another and hear the lesson continue.

Michelle had been reading books that began to push her thinking about the role of education for students, particularly Black students, including Paulo Freire's (1970) *Pedagogy of the Oppressed*, Carter G. Woodson's (1990) *The Mis-education of the Negro*, and W. E. B. Du Bois's (1903, 1920) *The Souls of Black Folk* and *The Souls of White Folk*. Through these readings, Michelle discovered long-held beliefs about the relationship between literacy and liberation, and she realized that although she could not change the curriculum, she could restructure the processes that governed her class. For instance, she began to question the need to take time away from instruction to answer students' requests to use the restroom, so she started allowing them to do so without asking. She followed the requirement for students to have a pass; they just did not have to ask for her permission. She felt that allowing her students to control their body movement demonstrated trust. For her, it was redirecting her focus to what really mattered, which was student learning, over having to worry about managing students' biological needs. As Michelle stated, "I try to really focus on what matters. Like what I have power over, and what I have power over is exercising content." This statement may sound innocuous; however, given the school's stringent requirements for following the rules, Michelle's actions presented a risk. The critical lesson here is about *trust*—trusting students to know what they need and putting in place mechanisms that empower agentive decision making.

Although this approach might be tricky for very young children, even they need to be afforded trust to know when to listen to their bodies. Research by Elsner and Aschersleben (2003) demonstrates that infants as young as 8 months have an awareness of their bodily needs and children as young as 12 months exercise their ability to initiate and imitate behavior connected to evidenced desires. Therefore, if infants can exhibit the ability to exercise control over their bodies, it stands to reason school-age children possess the same ability. Although teachers may not be able to control the switching of classrooms or the lunch schedule, there is no need to send the draconian message that adults know better than children about their own biological or physiological needs. If we put students' need to control their own bodies in terms of Maslow's (1943) hierarchy of needs and within the scope of research conducted by Tapal and colleagues (2017), who found, through their use of a sense of agency scale (SoAS), connections between bodily control and a sense of agency, it is safe to say students' ability to know what they need biologically and to exercise the ability to meet their own needs is associated with a positive sense of agency. Tapal and his colleagues (2017) state, "A sense of positive agency (SoPA) is essentially feeling in control of one's body, mind, and environment" (pp. 7–8). What Michelle did evidences this research and was a critical first step in building students' agency.

From Michelle's decision we learn the following:

- Recognizing students' need to control their body is essential to building agency.
- Giving students opportunities to exercise their agency is an avenue toward empowerment.
- Creating opportunities for empowerment and agency can live alongside schoolwide policies and procedures.

What Can We Learn from an Alternative Educational Environment?

"It's the context, stupid" (Smagorinsky, 2018). In the article that includes this quote, Smagorinsky discusses the importance of learning context as a driver for student engagement and learning. The quote is particularly salient for our discussion, because context is the driver of how teachers do their jobs, which greatly influences how students learn.

A teacher I'll call Judah learned the importance of instructional power while teaching at an alternative school in Washington, D.C. Her school was designed as a last chance of sorts for students who had been disenfranchised by traditional educational environments. As Judah describes it, "The school really empowers students." Teachers have to follow district-mandated instructional standards, but they do not have a set curriculum, making this a school where teachers had Unfettered Curricular Autonomy. In addition to the curricular autonomy, students were allowed to direct their learning by choosing which classes they would attend, how long they would stay in that class, or whether they would attend the class at all. Students faced no express penalties if they chose not to attend a class. In spending time with Judah and learning about her learning context, I was reminded of the Summerhill School in England, a boarding school founded in 1921 and designed on a constructivist model that gave students full autonomy to make empowered educative decisions (Neill, 1995). Such decisions are unheard of in traditional settings.

Judah admitted that, having taught at a different school, the environmental change was a culture shock that forced her to take a deep look at how her assumptions about students and about her role as a teacher shaped the instructional decisions she made. It was quite jarring to spend time developing what she believed to be engaging lessons only to have students walk out of her class in the middle, come back later, or not at all. Her first responses to her students' abilities to be empowered enough to fully exercise their educational agency was to attempt the usual show of force: demand compliance and threaten punitive action or a call home. None of this worked. Students continued to show up and leave class when they wanted. It was not until she began to ask herself some critical questions about how she understood herself as a teacher that she changed her instructional practices in ways that shifted her students' class attendance and their willingness to stay for the learning.

In our conversations about the shift, Judah explained that the first and most challenging part was to reconsider her beliefs about what it meant to teach. She shared how she had followed her students' lead by recognizing what was going on when they left class versus when they chose to stay. Judah took stock by asking the following questions:

- What was I teaching when students left class?
- What was I teaching when students stayed in class?
- What do I think made them come back to class or stay away completely?

At the school where she had taught previously, Judah typically used computers as the primary tool for her instructional delivery. Now, at the alternative school, she realized her students were leaving class more often when she did this than when she used her paper-and-pencil exercises. It seemed her students preferred what would be considered traditional ways of engaging with content over more modern forms.

Please do not take this to mean technology is bad. This example simply demonstrates the need to pay close attention to the messages students send when we're working to get them to engage in learning. Judah said she became more flexible and balanced her use of computer-based materials with use of the paper-and-pencil materials her students preferred—and completed more often. She also learned her students preferred smaller chunks of material at a time as opposed to longer learning cycles. Learning from her students forced her to reconfigure her pedagogy to fit their needs. Although her students did not advocate for themselves in traditional ways, they did so by leaving the class. Leaving the class was a form of advocacy because it forced Judah to pay attention to when they stayed and when they left, opening her eyes to their needs.

Such was not the case with one of her colleagues who took a different approach. Her colleague taught math and also came from a more traditional school environment, where students were not allowed to leave class at will. Upon arriving at the alternative school, Judah's colleague used more traditional means, just as Judah had when she first arrived. There were referrals to the office for students, constant calls home with little response, and a rigid learning environment where students were expected to follow a set of rules designed to control how they learned and moved. As Judah described it, the teacher's need to control students' behavior did not work well. Students regularly left the class and at times would try to come to Judah's class. By not paying attention to the context and the students, Judah's colleague created a hostile environment (Dimension IV/Disenfranchising) because of an unwillingness to let go of held beliefs about how students should learn and present themselves in school. Judah's colleague was more invested in protecting a particular way of instructing than in watching and learning from students.

From this example we learn the following:

- Letting go of preconceived notions about how students should learn might be challenging, but it is necessary.
- Self-reflection and introspection are critical to making changes that will lead to student empowerment and agency development.
- Context is everything. What works in one environment may not work in another.
- Insisting on doing things the way they have always been done creates a hostile Dimension IV/Disenfranchising learning environment. Be flexible.

The Importance of Self-Examination

As you have moved through the exercises in this book, I hope the one thing you've noticed is that the move from Dimensions III (Protective) and IV (Disenfranchising) to Dimensions II (Agentive) and I (Empowering) requires work. The shift goes beyond a prescribed set of steps or a list of protocols. When I have talked with teachers and leaders about this topic and have asked them what it takes to move from a place of disenfranchisement or protecting one's power to building authentic student agency and empowerment, they shared the need for educators to do their own personal work. One leader explained it this way:

> I think one of the first steps is teachers need to do their own personal work. What I mean by personal work is . . . who you are, what are your identity markers, particularly centered in race. What are your identity markers, and how does that show up in the classroom? What impact does that have on how you teach and how you instruct students, because I don't think we think about that enough. The other piece is thinking about the identity markers of your students and what impact does that have on how you decide to make decisions for instruction in the classroom.

This leader's perspective on doing one's own personal work is exactly what the exercises in this book have been designed to do. If we as educators do not take the time to dig into our memory banks to bring up what may be lying dormant, we have little chance of making the kinds of changes needed to foster student empowerment and agency development. School is one of the primary places some students get to learn about self-advocacy, agency, and empowerment. If this learning is afforded to students as their educators engage in self-reflection and the necessary environmental changes take place, the benefits to students can be far-reaching. Conversely, if this learning is withheld from them due to teachers' inability or unwillingness to examine themselves, the harm can be lifelong.

As this leader shared, knowing who you are in regard to race—and I would add ethnicity and gender to her thoughts—is critical to recognizing how these elements of your identity shape your approach to teaching and learning. Also important is being tuned in to your background, family structure, ideas shared in your family, your own school experiences, and overall life experiences. It is easy to see how these factors, taken together, structure and control our teacher identities. As another leader I spoke to summed it up: "It takes awareness to become an agency-building teacher." Her point was that educators should be aware of themselves, an observation that harkens back to the need for self-examination.

The deep personal work must involve an understanding of your power paradigm. Unpacking how you understand your power ideology and the impact it is having on students creates the space for critical action. Unpacking does not mean the outcome will necessitate a wholesale change in your instructional practice. It will, however, make you aware of what you are doing and whether your practices authentically support and empower students or simply protect your leadership position or even create a disenfranchising environment.

As Judah spoke about her understanding of power, she shared (as teachers often do) an initial disbelief about herself as having power. Her perspective was that teachers do not necessarily believe they have power primarily because "they're looking at their relationship to the school as a whole, to administration, to districts." It is easy to see how teachers, looking at themselves in relation to a system, do not believe they are powerful, especially regarding their ability to make critical decisions. Going back to Anderson (1987), we know that teachers exercise power in their space of primary control: the classroom. Although it is true that teachers are part of an educational system, there is no mistaking the reality that within their locus of control, they wield tremendous power. Therefore, developing an understanding of one's power paradigm is critical.

Knowledge of one's paradigm is only a beginning. If such self-knowledge reveals a propensity toward positional and institutional protection—or worse, toward disenfranchising—but no action is taken to move toward authentic empowerment, the self-knowledge is insufficient. Action is necessary to move forward; it is the evidence of learning. Although there are no absolutes on how to move forward, the framework in Figure 8.1 will put you on the road to developing agency and building empowerment.

FIGURE 8.1

A Framework for Developing Agency and Building Empowerment in Students

Personal Work	• Identify your identity markers. • Know your core beliefs as a person and as an educator. • Understand how your background has shaped your ideologies, beliefs, and behaviors. • Recognize your cultural, racial, gender, and religious biases and prejudices.
Power Principles	• Know your power ideologies. • Understand how your power principles shape your personal decision making. • Understand how your power principles shape your instructional decision making.
Student Work	• Know your students' identity markers. • Explore their backgrounds and family values (for all grades). • Learn their core beliefs and burgeoning ideologies (for upper elementary school and above). • Understand how their identities, backgrounds, beliefs, values, etc., influence their approach to learning.
Environment	• Analyze the cultural dynamics of your classroom. • Examine the power dynamics of your classroom. • Understand how the relationship between your identity and your students' identity influences your instructional decision making. • Examine how you approach grading, especially with the use of rubrics.

Remember the opening quote: "You can. You should. And if you're brave enough to start, you will." Getting on this road is possible, is necessary, and requires a decision to be brave enough to face yourself.

Building Students' Language and Negotiating Skills

Exercising agency and moving toward empowerment requires a set of skills student must be expressly taught. Students need linguistic dexterity in order to navigate a world designed for them to be compliant. Equipping students with the right types of language frames will not only equip them in school; it will prepare them for life, where self-advocacy is a critical skill.

One of my favorite lessons in my English language arts class was on tone and mood. Students understood mood quite easily but always seemed to struggle a bit with tone. To get my students to understand tone, I would say, "Raise your hand if your mom ever said these words: 'Don't use that *tone* with me!'" Students usually laughed and raised their hands, signaling that their moms often admonished them for how they spoke.

Building students' skills starts with helping them get their language and tone right. You've heard the phrase "It's not what you say; it's how you say it." Tone is where many students get into trouble. The problem is not *what* they want or try to get adults to do; it's *how* they phrase their requests. Equipping students with knowledge about tone protects them from adults who have a Dimension III/Protective or Dimension IV/Disenfranchising instructional stance. The goal is not to get students to cower; rather, it is to help them recognize how important it is for them to understand how language can be a tool for exercising their agency toward empowerment.

Building students' negotiating skills is essential to fostering agency and empowerment. Providing frameworks for collaboration and conversation will help them build their skills and confidence.

It will also provide the protection that traditionally marginalized students need when facing teachers who have unresolved biases against students they do not believe deserve the right to advocate for themselves. Conversation frames are low-threat, effective ways to build students' skills because they are tied to instruction. The more opportunities students have to practice in authentic ways, the more likely they are to incorporate these language skills in other areas of their academic and even their personal lives. As students adopt more nuanced language skills, it is helpful to have them reflect on how the use of the language improved their communication and helped them advocate for themselves. Figure 8.2 provides a few frames to consider adding to your planning and teaching repertoire.

The figure shows just a few examples of how students' tone can lead to them being refused support even if what they are requesting is legitimate. Giving them the language frames to exercise their agency will support them as they move toward empowerment. The goal is not to have students become robotic forms of adultness or to use acceptable forms of school-sanctioned speech to make those deemed threatening more accepting. It's about helping them better understand that they can advocate for themselves by exercising their agency and making empowered decisions.

You may have students who know how to use their language to disarm adults; however, you likely have other students who try to speak up for themselves but whose language is judged based on adult-style preferences instead of an understanding of student needs. The language frames will help students who do not know how to use the language adults prefer, or how to negotiate to get their academic needs met. As students use these frames, be sure to engage them in reflection about how and when they used them, along with the results they were able to get—especially when outcomes are not what they expected. Students have to understand they are not guaranteed the outcome they want even when they use their language in agentive and empowering ways. They must, however, understand that

FIGURE 8.2

Conversation Frames to Help Students Improve Their
Language Skills

Student Language	Suggested Rephrasing
"I don't want to do that."	"Would it be OK with you if I think of a different way to do this assignment?"
"I'm not feelin' this."	"I have another way to think about this. Would it be OK if I try it?"
"Why are we doing this?"	"I'm not clear on why we're doing this. Can you help me understand the purpose?"
"This is not fair. I never get called on."	"Can we talk? When I'm trying to participate, it feels like you ignore me."
"I want the ____ role. I'm better at it."	"Would it be OK if I took the role of ____? I really enjoy doing that kind of work and have been told I'm good at it."
"I'm not working in that group. They don't do their work."	"I really want to do well on this assignment/task/project. Is it possible to be placed with a different group of students?"
"I'm not sitting here."	"It's important to me to be able to do my work, and sitting where you placed me would be a distraction. Would you be willing to reseat me?"
"This is not enough time to do all this work."	"Is it possible to have more time to complete this assignment/task/project?"

language is a key element in building their agency and empowerment skills. Reflection will support them as they develop their confidence.

In addition to advocating for themselves regarding their assignments and collaborative relationships, students also need to understand how to navigate hostile environments where teacher bias creates stress and frustration, and they have to ensure their own academic and personal safety. Students need skills to navigate covert and overt forms of bias that seep out in adults' language and actions. They have to better understand how language can protect them from the adverse effects of adults' unrecognized biases and "isms." This understanding is particularly important for those whose school experiences have been marked by low academic expectations paired with high expectations for negative behavior.

As your class becomes more agentive and empowering, students may share with you their experiences with teachers demonstrating Protective and Disenfranchising instructional power. Preparing them with a framework to organize their thinking and responses, like the one in Figure 8.3, will help them better navigate their world and arm them with critical skills to reduce the stress and frustration caused by being in a hostile environment. You can use it with students as you learn about their experiences. The framework will offer you both a way to process what they are experiencing from your colleagues.

At the same time, you have to be ready to deal with the fact that many of your students may be experiencing hostile learning environments with colleagues you may respect and believe to be anything other than student-centered, let alone biased. You must also be ready to listen to your students and resist the urge to dismiss their concerns and go into your own form of Dimension III/Protective mode.

Students must develop the ability to make sense of their environments through analysis and inquiry before they employ critical actions. Reflection is essential because it will support them as they strengthen their agency and empowerment skills. Reflection can help students better understand how they process environments and respond in the future, especially in cases where further adult intervention becomes necessary. Students, especially Black students, have to know it is OK to involve adults when situations become more than they can handle on their own. They have to learn that involving the adults in their lives is its own form of exercising agency and being empowered; all too often, they are left defenseless because they don't realize the importance of allowing adults to help them.

FIGURE 8.3

A Framework to Help Students Deal with Teacher Bias and Prejudice

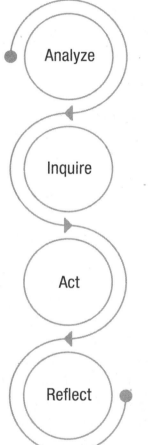

Analyze

Read and listen to the environment.
How is language used? Who gets to speak, participate, etc.? How do teachers and students get to use language?

Inquire

Ask critical questions to gain knowledge and meaning about the learning environment.
Is what you're experiencing a pattern? For whom?

Act

Use language as a tool to self-advocate and engage. *Think about ways to use language to understand, engage, and advocate for change.*

Reflect

Track responses and outcomes. *What changes have been noticed as a result of acting? What has been learned as a result of analyzing, inquiring, and acting? What further actions are needed? Does the environment require adult intervention?*

Guardrails to Support Students on Their Journey

Supporting students into agency and empowerment requires concerted effort. Educators must have a clear sense of their own power principles and paradigms, and know how to get students to understand that they have a right and responsibility to self-advocate. As stated earlier, students must be explicitly taught about agency and empowerment. They need learning situations that create opportunities to build the agency that leads to empowerment and the ability to make proper decisions for themselves. They must learn how to engage with others as well as how to exercise their agency in environments where adults are not prepared for or allow students to self-advocate.

Developing students' agency and empowerment is not about letting them do whatever they want or being one of the cool teachers who befriend their students but do not hold high academic and social expectations for them. Nor is it about expecting students to inherently *know* how to advocate for themselves or that they even have the right to do so. This reality is especially true for students who are in rigid, rule-centered educational environments. It is even more true for students of color, especially Black students whose attempts at self-advocacy have been met with adverse reactions from their teachers (Reeves, 2021).

A former colleague contacted me because she wanted support with helping her teachers become less rigid in their instructional practices. She was a coach at a school that focused on project-based learning. Her concern was that her teachers were engaging students in projects that focused on international issues, such as helping the community understand the plight of countries experiencing water shortages. The local paper had published articles celebrating the "water walks" students and their teachers organized to demonstrate and raise money for developing countries in need of water wells.

Although my colleague appreciated the work her teachers had led and the students had accomplished, she was concerned students were not developing a sense of their agency and empowerment to influence their local environment. She asked me to develop a professional development session to help teachers learn ways to develop student agency. As this coach and I discussed how to support teacher learning, my first question to her was "Are your teachers prepared for students to practice their newfound agency on *them*?" With hesitation, she replied in the negative, but then she asked me to explain what I meant.

Moving students toward agency and empowerment requires teachers be prepared for students to practice their skills on them. Students learn about agency in a variety of ways, and teachers use a variety of strategies to help them (Zeiser et al., 2018). They may learn about personal agency at home but not connect it to having academic agency at school where they can question and self-advocate. Learning that agency can be applied in school settings where they are able to self-advocate for their academic needs will likely mean students will practice this skill with the teacher who was willing to move them in this direction. Teachers must be prepared for this and think through how to respond as students grow their skills.

This preparation for a response requires clarity about your power paradigm. It is unrealistic to expect students will practice their skills in every other environment and skip the place at school where they initially learned their agency gives them responsibility over their academic lives. Students are likely to feel most comfortable with the educator brave enough to peel back the layers of how school works. They are likely to focus their attention on skill development where they feel most academically and socially safe at school. Students might focus on classroom procedures and assignments, and begin to notice and react to subtle biases they may have not noticed earlier.

Teachers must also rethink how they characterize what has been traditionally deemed "defiant" and "disrespectful" behavior. Go back to the example about my son. He was *asked* if he wanted to do something. He responded to his teacher based on her actual language, not the hidden language. Because he chose to say, "No, I don't want to go back and check my work," his teacher characterized him as defiant. Now let's be clear: there are times when students defy adults. This was not one of those instances. This was an instance of a child understanding the difference between being told to do something and being given the option to do something. This was an instance of a child exercising his agency and the adult being ill-prepared. Preparation necessitates intentionality, planning, and reflection. Think of it as a cycle, as shown in Figure 8.4.

FIGURE 8.4

The Cycle of Preparation for Student Empowerment

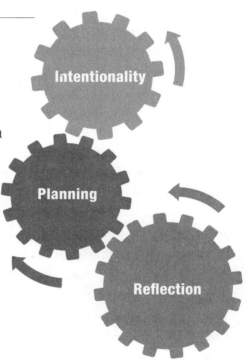

Intentionality is crucial as you begin to prepare for student empowerment. First you must understand and come to terms with your power paradigm, intentionally choosing to make a shift in your practice.

Planning allows you to build a classroom culture and learning experiences where students deliberately learn about power, agency, and empowerment and how to engage these effectively on their own behalf.

Reflection means you will continually ask yourself these critical questions:

- What additional learning do I need to do to deepen my knowledge/understanding?
- What did I intend?
- What did my students demonstrate?

- How are my students using their power and agency?
- How am I supporting them toward empowerment?
- How am I engaging with my colleagues?

Being intentional, developing specific plans, and reflecting on your practice is a critical first step in having the right guardrails to move your students toward agency and empowerment. Much of the work can occur within a well-crafted lesson. This involves more than the gradual-release portion of the "I do/We do/You do" format. Having guardrails means you have developed a sense of your power paradigm, you understand your classroom culture, and you look for specific ways to teach your students about their power and the responsibility they have to exercise their agency. It also means your lessons may be different. You will need to examine student interactions by asking the following questions and taking the following actions:

Collaboration
- How are students organized to work with their peers?
- How often are students afforded opportunities to determine their working groups?
- Help students understand the value of choosing partners wisely by doing the following:
  - Discuss the characteristics of effective partnerships and guide them in developing such characteristics.
  - Hold them accountable for choosing effective partners.
  - Hold partnerships accountable for productive work.

Participation
- How has participation shifted to allow more voices?
  - Where is the starting point of student participation?
  - When are students more actively participating?
- How are students participating?
- Which students are challenging tasks assigned, expectations communicated, requests, and so on?
- How are students expressing dissent?
  - What are you learning from students through their dissent?
  - How are you responding to students' dissent?
- How might you support students who tend toward compliance?

- Which students are more compliant? Critical questions for your students who tend toward compliance:
  ○ What questions do you have about what's being asked of you?
  ○ What part of the lesson, assignment, or project would you prefer *not* to have to do?
  ○ What suggestions do you have that would make this lesson, assignment, or project more effective, productive, and enjoyable?

Looking critically at how you structure collaboration and prepare for student voice is necessary to help you understand where in the learning process students tend to be silent or silently rebel by underperforming, complaining, or refusing to complete tasks or engage in the work you have planned.

Another point to keep in mind is this: although you might be on a journey to foster student empowerment and agency, your colleagues might not. Students must be prepared for those classrooms where their agency is not welcomed. As you move forward, a critical conversation you owe your students is how to engage with a teacher who may be in Dimension III/Protective or Dimension IV/Disenfranchising. If students walk into these classrooms ready to exercise their agency but are ill-prepared for the potential reaction, you have done them a disservice. As you have read, teachers in these dimensions hold to more traditional norms about teacher-student relationships and are likely to react negatively when students appear to challenge their authority. Part of preparing students is alerting them to the risks involved in exercising their agency with adults who do not believe students deserve or have the right to do so. There are no magic bullets available to protect students from adults who hold archaic perspectives on what students should and should not be able to do as owners of their learning. However, I propose the following as a start:

- **Be honest.** Let your students know that not every adult is ready for empowered students who know they have agency.

- **Be direct.** Let students know they could face consequences if they choose to exercise their agency with an adult who does not believe they should be doing so.
- **Be supportive.** When one of your students receives a negative reaction from an adult, help them to reflect on the situation; provide feedback.
- **Be ready.** Be prepared to address your colleagues on behalf of your students. You will need to be your students' advocate outside your classroom, and at times you may even have to step in and stop a referral or some other adult reaction to protect your students from Dimension III/Protective and IV/Disenfranchising adults.

Guardrails are really about ensuring your students understand that they have a responsibility to own their learning, advocate for their learning needs, and prepare for their future. As one leader stated, "This is about getting kids ready for their life." Think of empowerment and agency development as the most critical life skills educators can bring out of their students. There will always be content to learn and rules to follow; however, the degree to which students are prepared to navigate the world around them requires them to know they have a right and responsibility to advocate for their needs.

It might seem scary to step back from the stage, but I challenge you to step up—that is, step up your self-knowledge. Step up your student knowledge and step up to being committed to a set of ideologies and practices that support students as they grow in their ability to understand how to become self-advocates in systems that are not necessarily designed for them to do so.

Concluding Thoughts

When I first thought about the many decisions teachers get to make, it occurred to me that such decision making carries a lot of weight.

When I reflect on my own practices as a classroom teacher, I remember those times when I made decisions in my own best interest instead of for my students. In my work with many teachers, I am struck by how many feel powerless because they do what Judah said she had done: see themselves in relation to their school district and state.

One thing is certain: teachers wield tremendous power in each decision they make. As one of my colleagues shared, "Having Unfettered Curricular Autonomy is not always good; it creates unevenness." In my quest to better understand how educators thought about power, this statement struck me because there is a common belief that if only teachers could do what they wanted, students would do better. Nothing could be further from the truth. There is just as much potential for the misuse of instructional power in classrooms where teachers have Unfettered Curricular Autonomy as in places where they have Restricted Curricular Autonomy. The goal is to ensure students are building the skills *they* need to navigate *their* world. It is the responsibility of educators to foster the type of learning that will make this happen.

To get students more fully engaged in their learning, teachers have to do a lot of learning themselves about the personal barriers they put in place that hinder students' ability to become empowered, agency-practicing individuals. This effort starts with educators taking a hard look at themselves to more fully understand who they are as people and how that shapes their instruction and their interactions with their students.

The dimensions presented in this book offer one way to begin the work of fostering empowered environments of authentic learning. As you worked on the Pause to Reflect activities, I hope you were able to gain insight into yourself and your decision-making processes in ways that made room for critical change. I hope you were able to see changes in how your students responded when you decided to restructure the learning environment so they could learn more about what it means to be empowered and how to effectively exercise their agency.

This journey into helping students become empowered, agency-exercising people is scary because it requires you to see yourself in ways you might not have before. But if you make the decision to embark on this journey, you will be successful—and your students will, too.

ACKNOWLEDGMENTS

Like most people who have enough to say and are brave enough to turn their thoughts into a book, I must acknowledge those for whom this book would not be possible. First, my family, especially my husband Bob and children Aerin and Robert. Your eyes and thoughtful insight helped challenge and shape my thinking. You gave me encouragement, asked all the right questions, conducted research, kept me on track, and let me know this was possible. I am eternally grateful! Thank you!!

To my NC crew and brain trust, y'all know who you are. Thank you for always checking on my progress and keeping me laughing. We are framily!

To Chrystal, Jalinda, Mariama, and Kathy, thank you for lending your stories. You brought our many discussions to life. I so appreciate your friendship, thoughtfulness, and support.

Finally, to Susan and Liz at ASCD, thank you for your confidence in my topic and its ability to support educators, your patience with me and deadlines, and most of all your thoughtful eyes and partnership. It has been a pleasure to have you work with me on this first project. It is my hope we get to do it again.

REFERENCES

Aboud, F. E. (2008). A social-cognitive developmental theory of prejudice. In S. M. Quintata & C. McKown (Eds.), *Handbook of race, racism, and the developing child* (pp. 55–71). Wiley.

Allensworth, E. M., & Easton, J. Q. (2005). *The on-track indicator as a predictor of high school graduation.* UC Consortium on School Research, University of Chicago.

Allensworth, E. M., & Easton, J. Q. (2007). *What matters for staying on-track and graduating in Chicago public high schools.* UC Consortium on School Research, University of Chicago.

Alsubaie, M. A. (2015). Hidden curriculum as one of current issue of curriculum. *Journal of Education and Practice, 6*(33), 125–128.

Anderson, L. W. (1987). The decline of teacher autonomy: Tears or cheers? *International Review of Education, 33*(3), 357–373.

Apple, M. W. (1982). *Education and power.* Routledge.

Ball, D. L. (1992). *Implementing the NCTM standards: Hopes and hurdles* (Issue paper 92-2). National Center for Research on Teacher Learning, Michigan State University.

Ball, D. L. (2018). *Just dreams and imperatives: The power of teaching in the struggle for public education.* Paper presented at the annual meeting of the American Educational Research Association (AERA), New York.

Bishop, R. S. (1990). Windows and mirrors: Children's books and parallel cultures. In *Celebrating literacy: Proceedings of the 14th Annual Reading Conference at California State University* (pp. 3–12).

Bonsor, K., & Chandler, N. (2001). How black boxes work. Howstuffworks.com. https://science.howstuffworks.com/transport/flight/blackbox

Bridges, B. K., Awokoya, J. T., & Messano, F. (2012). *Done to us, not with us: African American parent perceptions of K–12 education.* Frederick D. Patterson Research Institute, UNCF.

Bryan, N. (2017). White teachers' role in sustaining the school-to-prison pipeline: Recommendations for teacher education. *Urban Review, 49,* 326–345.

Civil Rights Data Collection (CRDC). (2014). Data snapshot: School discipline. Issue Brief 1. www.crdc.org

Cornelius, L. L., & Herrenkohl, L. R. (2004). Power in the classroom: How the classroom environment shapes students' relationships with each other and with concepts. *Cognition and Instruction, 22*(4), 467–498.

Delgado, R. (2007). The myth of upward mobility. *University of Pittsburgh Law Review, 68*(4), 879.

Delpit, L. (1995). *Other people's children: Cultural conflict in the classroom.* New Press.

Delpit, L. (2012). *Multiplication is for White people: Raising expectations for other people's children.* New Press.

DeMitchell, T. A. (2015). School uniforms in New Hampshire public schools: Hype or hope? (Policy brief). University of New Hampshire Department of Education.

Devereaux, M. D. (2015). *Teaching about dialect variations and language in secondary English classrooms: Power, prestige, and prejudice.* Routledge.

Dilliard, J. L. (1975). *All-American English.* Random House.

Dixon, D., Griffin, A., & Teoh, M. (2019). *If you listen, we will stay: Why teachers of color leave and how to disrupt teacher turnover.* The Education Trust.

Douglas, B., Lewis, C. W., Douglas, A., Scott, M. E., & Garrison-Wade, D. (2008). The impact of White teachers on the achievement of Black students: An exploratory qualitative analysis. *Educational Foundations, 22*(1–2), 47–62.

Downey, D. B., & Pribesh, S. (2004). When race matters: Teachers' evaluations of students' classroom behavior. *Sociology of Education, 77*(4), 267–282.

Drydyk, J. (2013). Empowerment, agency, and power. *Journal of Global Ethics, 9*(3), 249–262.

Du Bois, W. E. B. (1903). *The souls of Black folk.* Random House.

Du Bois, W. E. B. (1920). *The souls of White folk.* In W. E. B. Du Bois, *Darkwater: Voices from within the veil* (pp. 29–52). Schocken.

Dunn, A. H. (2018). Leaving a profession after it's left you: Teachers' public resignation letters as resistance amidst neoliberalism. *Teachers College Record, 120*(9), 1–34.

Elsner, B., & Aschersleben, G. (2003). Do I get what you get? Learning about the effects of self-performed and observed actions in infancy. *Consciousness and Cognition, 12*(4), 732–751.

Feldman, J. (2018). *Grading for equity: What it is, why it matters, and how it can transform schools and classrooms.* Corwin.

Freire, P. (1970). *The pedagogy of the oppressed.* Continuum.

Freire, P. (1974). *Education for critical consciousness.* Bloomsbury.

Freire, P. (1985). *The politics of education: Culture, power, and liberation.* Bergin & Garvey.

García, E., & Weiss, E. (2019). *Low relative pay and high incidence of moonlighting play a role in the teacher shortage, particularly in high-poverty schools.* The Third Report in "The Perfect Storm in the Teacher Labor Market" Series. Economic Policy Institute.

Gholson, M. L., & Wilkes, C. E. (2017). (Mis)taken identities: Reclaiming identities of the "collective Black" in mathematics education research through an exercise in Black specificity. *Review of Research in Education, 41*(1), 228–251.

Gilliam, W. S., Maupin, A. N., Reyes, C. R., Accavitti, M., & Shic, F. (2016). *Do early educators' implicit biases regarding sex and race relate to behavior expectations and recommendations of preschool expulsions and suspensions?* [Research study brief]. Yale University Child Study Center.

Giroux, H. (1984) Rethinking the language of schooling. *Language Arts, 61*(1), 33–40.

Giroux, H. A., & Penna, A. N. (1979). Social education in the classroom: The dynamics of the hidden curriculum. *Theory and Research in Social Education, 7*(1), 21–42.

Gould, S. J. (1981). *The mismeasure of man.* W. W. Norton.

Gramsci, A. (1971). The modern prince. *Selections from the prison notebooks.* International Press.

Gray, S. M. (2016). Saving the lost boys: Narratives on discipline disproportionality. *Educational Leadership and Administration: Teaching and Program Development, 27,* 53–80.

Griffin, A. (2018). *Our stories, our struggles, our strengths: Perspectives and reflections from Latino teachers.* Education Trust.

Hart, B. & Risley, T. R. (2003). The early catastrophe: The 30 million word gap by age 3. *American Educator,* 27(1), 4–9.

Heath, S.B. (1992). American English: Quest for a model. In B. B. Kachru (Ed.), *The other language: English across cultures* (2nd ed.). University of Illinois Press.

Horton, M., & Freire, P. (1990). We make the road by walking: Conversations on education and social change. Philadelphia: Temple University Press.

Howard, E. (2015). *African American parents' perceptions of public school: African American parents' involvement in their children's education.* Electronic Theses and Dissertations. Paper 2575. https://dc.etsu.edu/etd/2575

Howard, G. R. (2016). *We can't teach what we don't know: White teachers, multicultural schools* (2nd ed.). Teachers College Press.

Howard, T. C., & Reynolds, R. (2008). Examining parent involvement in reversing the underachievement of African American students in middle-class schools. *Education Foundations*, *22*(1–2), 79–98.

Inniss-Thompson, M. (2017). *Summary of discipline data for girls in US public schools: An analysis from the 2013–14 US Department of Education, Office of Civil Rights Data Collection.* National Black Women's Justice Institute.

James, G. G. M. (2017). *Stolen legacy: Greek philosophy is stolen Egyptian philosophy.* Simon & Schuster.

Jefferson, T. (1787). *Notes on the state of Virginia.* John Stockdale Books.

Kahne, H. (1992). American English: From a colonial substandard to a prestige language. In B. B. Kachru (Ed.), *The other tongue: English across cultures* (2nd ed.). University of Illinois Press.

Kendi, I. X. (2016). *Stamped from the beginning. The definitive history of racist ideas in America.* Nation Books.

Klein, A. (2021, December 6). 1,500 decisions a day (at least!): How teachers cope with a dizzying array of questions. *Education Week.* https://www.edweek.org/teaching-learning/1-500-decisions-a-day-at-least-how-teachers-cope-with-a-dizzying-array-of-questions/2021/12

Kohl, H. (2002). Topsy-turvies: Teacher talk and student talk. In L. Delpit & J. K. Dowdy (Eds.), *The skin that we speak: Thoughts on language and culture in the classroom* (pp. 145–161). New Press.

Kundu, A. (2020). *The power of student agency: Looking beyond grit to close the opportunity gap.* Teachers College Press.

Lambert, L. (2006, May 9). Half of teachers quit in 5 years. *Washington Post*, A7.

Liiv, K. (2015). *Defiance, insubordination, and disrespect: Perceptions of power in middle school discipline.* Doctoral dissertation, Harvard Graduate School of Education.

Martin, D. B. (2012). Learning mathematics while Black. *Education Foundations*, *26*(1–2), 47–66.

Martin, J., & Smith, J. (2017). Subjective discipline and the social control of Black girls in pipeline schools. *Journal of Urban Learning, Teaching, and Research,* 63–72.

Maslow, A. H. (1943). A theory of human motivation. *Psychological Review, 50*(4), 370–396.

McConachie, S. M., & Petrosky, A. R. (2009). *Content matters: A disciplinary literacy approach to improving learning.* Jossey-Bass.

McEvoy, A. (2005). *Teachers who bully students: Patterns and policy implications.* Paper presented at the Hamilton Fish Institute's Persistently Safe Schools Conference.

McGee, E., & Martin, D. (2011). "You would not believe what I have to go through to prove my intellectual value!" Stereotype management among academically successful mathematics and engineering students. *American Education Research Journal, 48*(6), 1347–1389.

McNamee, S. J., & Miller, R. K. (2004). The meritocracy myth. *Sociation Today, 2*(1), 1–12.

Meek, A. P. (2009). School discipline "as part of the teaching process": Alternative and compensatory education required by the state's interest in keeping kids in schools. *Yale Law and Policy Review, 28*(1), 155–185.

Monroe, C. R. (2005). Understanding the discipline gap through a cultural lens: Implications for the education of African American students. *Intercultural Education, 16*(4), 317–330.

Morris, M. W. (2016). *Pushout: The criminalization of Black girls in schools.* The New Press.

National Research Council. (2011). *High school dropout, graduation, and completion rates: Better data, better measures, better decisions.* National Academies Press.

Neill, A. S. (1995). *Summerhill school: A new view of childhood.* St. Martin's Griffin.

Nyberg, D. (1981). *Power over power.* Cornell University Press.

Orr, B., Thompson, C., & Thompson, D. E. (1999). Pre-service teachers perceived success of classroom management strategies. *Journal of Family and Consumer Sciences Education, 17*(1).

Pace, J. L., & Hemmings, A. (2007). Understanding authority in classrooms: A review of theory, ideology, and research. *Review of Educational Research, 77*(1), 4–27.

Parker, F., Novak, J., & Bartell, T. (2017). To engage students, give them meaningful choices in the classroom. *Phi Delta Kappan, 99*(2), 37–41.

Patrick, K., Socol, R. A., & Morgan, I. (2020). *Inequities in advanced coursework.* Education Trust. https://edtrust.org/resource/inequities-in-advanced-coursework/

Perry, T., Steele, C., & Hilliard, A. (2003). *Young, gifted and black: Promoting high achievement among African-American students.* Beacon.

Raney, M. (1997). Technos interview: Jeff Howard. *Technos, 6*(2), 4–11.

Reed Marshall, T. (2016). Problematizing teacher authority to uncover and address the reality of teacher bullies. In A. F. Osanloo, C. Reed, & J. P. Schwartz (Eds.), *Creating and negotiating collaborative spaces for socially just, anti-bullying interventions for K–12 schools* (pp. 257–276). Information Age Publishing.

Reed Marshall, T., & Seawood, C. (2019). How power reveals and directs teacher language ideologies with high-achieving African American students in a secondary English classroom. In M. D. Devereaux & C. C. Palmer (Eds.), *Teaching language variation in the classroom* (pp. 138–146). Routledge.

Reeves, T. (2021). *Defiance, disrespect, and insubordination: Disciplinary power in school discipline policies and practices; a Foucauldian synoptic text.* Unpublished doctoral dissertation, George Washington University.

Rigby, K. (2001). Health consequences of bullying and its prevention in schools. In J. Juvonen & S. Graham (Eds.), *Peer harassment in school: The plight of the vulnerable and victimized* (pp. 310–331). Guilford.

Sen, A. (1985). Well-being, agency, and freedom: The Dewey lectures. *Journal of Philosophy, 82*(4), 169–221.

Seneca Keyes, T. (2019). A qualitative inquiry: Factors that promote classroom belonging and engagement among high school students. *School Community Journal*, 29(1), 171–200.

Skiba, R., & Losen, D. (2016). From reaction to prevention: Turning the page on school discipline. *American Educator, 39*(4), 4–11/44.

Skiba, R., & Peterson, R. (2000). School discipline at the crossroads: From zero tolerance to early response. *Exceptional Children, 66*(3), 335–347.

Sleeter, C. (2008). Preparing White teachers for diverse students. In M. Cochran-Smith, S. Feiman-Nemser, J. McIntyre, & K. Demers, (Eds.), *Handbook for teacher education*. Routledge.

Smagorinsky, P. (2018). Literacy in teacher education: "It's the context, stupid." *Journal of Literacy Research, 50*(3), 281–303.

Stambaugh, T., & Ford, D. Y. (2014). Microaggressions, multiculturalism, and gifted individuals who are Black, Hispanic, or low income. *Journal of Counseling & Development, 93*(2), 192–201.

Starck, J. G., Riddle, T., Sinclair, S., & Warikoo. N. (2020). Teachers are people too: Examining the racial bias of teachers compared to other American adults. *Educational Researcher, 49*(4), 273–284.

Steele, C. (2010). *Whistling Vivaldi: How stereotypes affect us and what we can do*. W. W. Norton.

Stubbs, M. (2002). Some basic sociolinguistic concepts. In L. Delpit & J. K. Dowdy (Eds.), *The skin that we speak: Thoughts on language and culture in the classroom* (pp. 65–86). New Press.

Tapal, A., Oren, E., Dar, R., & Eitam, B. (2017). The sense of agency scale: A measure of consciously perceived control over one's mind, body, and the immediate environment. *Frontiers in Psychology, 8,* 1552.

Tatum, B. D. (1997). *Why are all the black kids sitting together in the cafeteria? And other conversations about race*. Basic Books.

Terry, M. L., & Baer, A. M. (2012). Bully teachers. *American School Board Journal, 199*(12), 24–25.

The New Teacher Project (TNTP). (2018). *The opportunity myth: What students can show us about how school is letting them down—and how to fix it*. TNTP.

Toldson, I. A. (2019). *No BS (bad stats): Black people need people who believe in Black people enough not to believe every bad thing they hear about Black people*. Brill.

Twemlow, S. W., Fonagy, P., Sacco, F. C., & Brethour Jr., J. R. (2006). Teachers who bully students: A hidden trauma. *International Journal of Social Psychiatry, 52*(3), 187–198.

Wexler, N. (2020, February 28). Achievement gaps increase the longer kids stay in school: Here's why. *Forbes*. https://www.forbes.com/sites/nataliewexler /2020/05/17/achievement-gaps-increase-the-longer-kids-stay-in-school-heres-why/?sh=1551b43d36b5

White, B. A. (2017). The invisible victims of the school-to-prison pipeline: Understanding black girls, school push-out, and the impact of the Every Student Succeeds Act. *William & Mary Journal of Women & the Law, 3*. https://scholarship.law.wm.edu/wmjowl/vol24/iss3/8

Williams, H. A. (2005). *Self-taught: African American education in slavery and freedom*. University of North Carolina Press.

Williams, R. (1977). *Marxism and literature*. Oxford University Press.

Wolf, Z. (2019). Why teacher strikes are touching every part of America. CNN Politics. https://www.cnn.com/2019/02/23/politics/teacher-strikes-politics

Woodson, C. G. (1990). *The mis-education of the Negro*. Africa World.

Wright, B. L., & Counsell, S. (2018). *The brilliance of Black boys: Cultivating school success in the early grades*. Teachers College Press.

Zeiser, K., Scholz, C., & Cirks, V. (2018). *Maximizing student agency: Implementing and measuring student-centered learning practices*. American Institutes for Research.

INDEX

The letter *f* following a page locator denotes a figure.

217

ABOUT THE AUTHOR

 **Tanji Reed Marshall,** PhD, is a nationally recognized and sought-after expert on educational equity and educational leadership. She has more than two decades of experience in advancing practice on behalf of students of color, those experiencing economic uncertainty, and those perpetually left on the margins of the education system.

Reed Marshall partners with states, school districts, schools, and education organizations to solve complex issues related to educational equity, improve educational leadership, stem the effects of systemic inequity, and improve teacher practice and student outcomes. She has presented at international and national conferences on topics related to educational equity and power dynamics, curriculum development, literacy, critical literacy, teacher development, and authentic pedagogies.

Additionally, Reed Marshall is the director of P–12 practice at the Education Trust, a nonprofit educational equity and advocacy think tank in Washington, D.C. In this role, she works to advance understanding and implementation of promising practices to ensure every child has access to and receives the excellent equitable education they deserve.

Reed Marshall earned her doctorate in curriculum and instruction from Virginia Polytechnic Institute and State University (Virginia Tech), her master's in English education from the University of North Carolina at Charlotte, and a bachelor's degree in psychology from Boston College.

Related ASCD Resources

At the time of publication, the following resources were available (ASCD stock numbers in parentheses).

Becoming the Educator They Need: Strategies, Mindsets, and Beliefs for Supporting Male Black and Latino Students by Robert Jackson (#119010)

Building Equity: Policies and Practices to Empower All Learners by Dominique Smith, Nancy Frey, Ian Pumpian, and Douglas Fisher (#117031)

Cultivating Joyful Learning Spaces for Black Girls: Insights into Interrupting School Pushout by Monique W. Morris (#121004)

Cultural Competence Now: 56 Exercises to Help Educators Understand and Challenge Bias, Racism, and Privilege by Vernita Mayfield (#118043)

Culture, Class, and Race: Constructive Conversations That Unite and Energize Your School and Community by Brenda CampbellJones, Shannon Keeny, and Franklin CampbellJones (#118010)

Five Practices for Equity-Focused School Leadership by Sharon I. Radd, Gretchen Givens Generett, Mark Anthony Gooden, and George Theoharis (#120008)

The Innocent Classroom: Dismantling Racial Bias to Support Students of Color by Alexs Pate (#120025)

Keeping It Real and Relevant: Building Authentic Relationships in Your Diverse Classroom by Ignacio Lopez (#117049)

Literacy Is Liberation: Working Toward Justice Through Culturally Relevant Teaching by Kimberly N. Parker (#122024)

Restoring Students' Innate Power: Trauma-Responsive Strategies for Teaching Multilingual Newcomers by Louise El-Yaafouri (#122004)

Teaching with Empathy: How to Transform Your Practice by Understanding Your Learners by Lisa Westman (#121027)

What We Say and How We Say It Matter: Teacher Talk That Improves Student Learning and Behavior by Mike Anderson (#119024)

For up-to-date information about ASCD resources, go to www.ascd.org. You can search the complete archives of *Educational Leadership* at www.ascd.org/el. To contact us, send an email to member@ascd.org or call 1-800-933-2723 or 703-578-9600.

WHOLE CHILD
TENETS

The ASCD Whole Child approach is an effort to transition from a focus on narrowly defined academic achievement to one that promotes the long-term development and success of all children. Through this approach, ASCD supports educators, families, community members, and policymakers as they move from a vision about educating the whole child to sustainable, collaborative actions.

Understanding Your Instructional Power relates to the **safe** and **supported** tenets.

*For more about the ASCD Whole Child approach, visit **www.ascd.org/wholechild.***

1 HEALTHY
Each student enters school healthy and learns about and practices a healthy lifestyle.

2 SAFE
Each student learns in an environment that is physically and emotionally safe for students and adults.

3 ENGAGED
Each student is actively engaged in learning and is connected to the school and broader community.

4 SUPPORTED
Each student has access to personalized learning and is supported by qualified, caring adults.

5 CHALLENGED
Each student is challenged academically and prepared for success in college or further study and for employment and participation in a global environment.